by Joanne Settel, PhD

illustrated by Steve Björkman

Atheneum Books for Young Readers
atheneum New York London Toronto Sydney New Delhi

Your Amazing DIGESTION from MOUTH through Intestine

atheneum

ATHENEUM BOOKS FOR YOUNG READERS
An imprint of Simon & Schuster Children's Publishing Division
1230 Avenue of the Americas, New York, New York 10020
Text copyright © 2019 by Joanne Settel
Illustrations copyright © 2019 by Steve Björkman
Special thanks to Dr. Dana Zalkin, MD, chief resident of internal medicine at NYU School of Medicine, for sharing her expertise and input.
For information about special discounts for bulk purchases, please contact Simon & Schuster Special Sales at 1-866-506-1949 or business@simonandschuster.com.
The Simon & Schuster Speakers Bureau can bring authors to your live event. For more information or to book an event, contact the Simon & Schuster Speakers Bureau at 1-866-248-3049 or visit our website at www.simonspeakers.com.
Book design by Debra Sfetsios-Conover
The text for this book was set in Archer Book.
The illustrations for this book were rendered in pen, ink, and watercolor.
Manufactured in China
0419 SCP
First Edition
10 9 8 7 6 5 4 3 2 1
Library of Congress Cataloging-in-Publication Data
Names: Settel, Joanne, author. | Björkman, Steve, illustrator.
Title: Your amazing digestion from mouth through intestine / by Joanne Settel, PhD ; illustrated by Steve Björkman.
Description: First edition. | New York : Atheneum Books for Young Readers, [2018] | "An imprint of Simon & Schuster Children's Publishing Division." | Audience: Ages 7–12. | Audience: Grades 4 to 6. | Includes bibliographical references and index.
Identifiers: LCCN 2017018015 | ISBN 9781481486880 (hardcover) | ISBN 9781481486897 (eBook)
Subjects: LCSH: Digestion—Juvenile literature. | Human physiology—Juvenile literature. | Children's questions and answers.
Classification: LCC QP145 .S37 2018 | DDC 612.3—dc23
LC record available at https://lccn.loc.gov/2017018015

CONTENTS

CONCLUSION

*(Note: first appearance of glossary words appear bold in the text.)

PART I
FROM TOP TO BOTTOM, MOVING THROUGH

Digestion's an amazing feat!
It transforms all the food you eat
so that the things on which you feed
get changed into the things you need.

To understand this, first, we'll see
how one food's special **chemistry**
provides the **building blocks** you turn
to **tissue** parts and **fuel** you burn.

And then we'll see how food bits go
down through each organ, nice and slow,
and watch the soupy, gooey paste
turn into **nutrients** and waste.

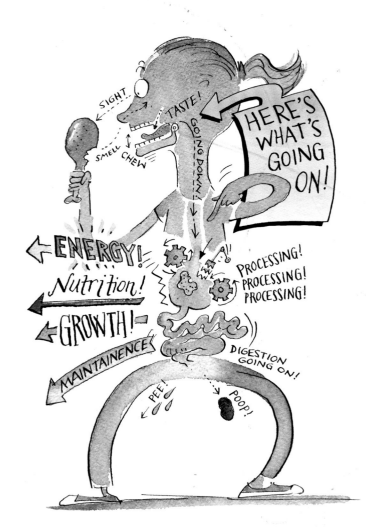

What Hides Inside a Pizza Slice?

The pizza that you ate last night
got rearranged with every bite.
That gooey cheese and sauce and bread
broke into nutrients instead.

Inside each slice, it turns out that
you'll find **carbs**, **proteins**, and some **fat**,
some **vitamins**, and **minerals**, too.
They'll soon become a part of you.

(a) The Carbohydrates (Carbs)

You'll get some **starches** from the crust:
large **carbohydrates**, which then must
be split to **glucose molecules**
that active **cells** can use as fuels.

The glucose carries **energy**,
and hungry cells can set it free.
Cells break down glucose bit by bit,
extracting fuel they need from it.

(b) The Proteins

You'll get some proteins from the cheese,
but you can't do a thing with these.
They're big, and not **absorbed** at all
by cells in the **intestines**' walls.

But every protein does contain
amino acids in a chain.
Digestion breaks each one of these
off from the chain so it's set free.

Then each small **compound** can pass through
your **small intestine**, right into
your blood and body's cells, where then
they're turned to proteins once again.

You use these proteins every day,
to sleep and work and run and play.
The list is long, but here's a few
of all the things your proteins do:

Strong, stretchy proteins are a part
of all your tissues, for a start:
they're in your skin; they're in your hair,
in bones, in blood. They're everywhere!

They **bind** your cells—they hold like glue—
to build your tissues; **organs**, too.
They help your muscles to **contract**
and let skin stretch and then spring back.

Proteins form **enzymes**, which cells need
to do the things they do with speed.
Like burning fuel for energy
or healing up an injury.

And there are **hormones** you create
from proteins; these help **regulate**
things like how cells grow and divide
and pull blood nutrients inside.

To sum it all up, you will find
that proteins stretch, contract, and bind,
and speed things up, and regulate.
All from that yummy cheese you ate!

(c) The Fats

Inside that cheese is lots of fat.
And fats are broken down so that
they form small bits—and nearly all
can pass through the intestine's wall.

Digested fats work very well
to help us grow each brand-new cell.
They keep us warm, and they can be
an extra source of energy.

Plus many fats form hormones, too.
These have a range of jobs to do.
Some change blood chemistry and flow,
and others make sex organs grow.

Your fat plays an important part
protecting organs, like your heart.
It holds digestive organs down
so there's less chance they'll slide around.

In sum, fats regulate and feed
our blood and cells when there's a need,
and warm and cushion to diffuse
the impact of a bump or bruise.

(d) The Vitamins and Minerals

Here are some other healthy things
that every slice of pizza brings.
Packed in the sauce and cheese and crust
are vitamins. These are a must!

There's A, six different Bs, and C;
There's K and D and also E.
A pizza can have all of these
(including all those different Bs)!

Now if you think that's all, it's not.
'Cause every slice of pizza's got
some minerals. Their presence counts,
though we need only small amounts.

There's iron, zinc, and calcium,
potassium, magnesium,
and sodium and phosphorus
in sauce and cheese and pizza crust.

These minerals are needed for
our skin, our bones, our **nerves**, and more.
Our eyes need them; they help us see!
They help our cells use energy.

To sum it up, we need them all—
the nutrients both big and small.
And isn't it so very nice
they're all in just one pizza slice?

COOL FACTS ABOUT NUTRITION IN PIZZA

- The vitamins and minerals we need are required in such tiny amounts that we call them "micronutrients" ("micro" means small). We measure these amounts in milligrams (mg). It takes around 2,260 mg of salt to fill one teaspoon, which is the current recommendation for the total amount of salt we should eat each day. (Most folks eat considerably more than that.) And our bodies require much, much less of many other nutrients. For example, we need around 80 mg of Vitamin C—just a sprinkle—and even less of the mineral zinc, 11 mg. Still, we must eat these teeny, tiny amounts of micronutrients every day to stay healthy.

- Though pizza is chock-full of nutrients, it has a downside. Whole-fat, white flour pizza has a lot of **calories**. And putting pepperoni or sausage on top adds even more. Low-fat, whole-wheat pizza topped with vegetables is a smart choice; it has fewer calories and extra nutrients. It's still yummy, while providing the healthiest pizza meal.

A Slice of Pizza Going Down

So what digestion's all about
is pulling your food's goodies out.
To get them out, though, food must go
through several organs in a row.

This pathway that the food moves through
includes the mouth; the **stomach**, too;
and both the small and **large intestines**.
All have key roles in digestion.

Plus off the path, two organs sit
that aid digestion quite a bit:
The **pancreas** makes enzymes, while
the **liver** makes a juice called **bile**.

Let's see what all these organs do
as what you eat gets pushed on through.
This section has the inside scoop:
from pizza pie to what we poop!

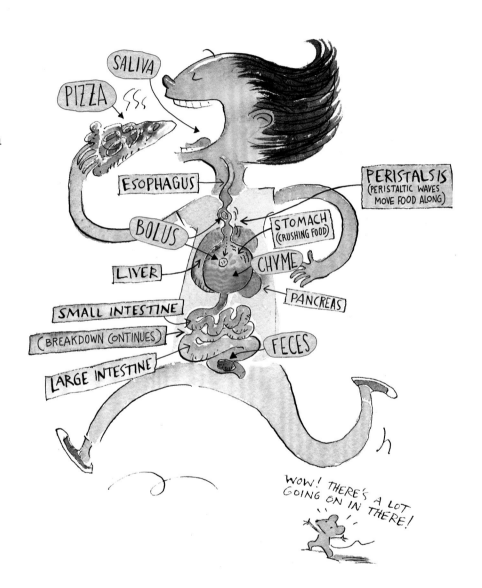

(a) Pizza in the Mouth: Chewing and Swallowing

The mouth's the place where you begin
to break down food that you take in.
Not just with teeth, which grind and chew,
but salivary enzymes, too.

The pizza's breakdown starts at once.
You take a bite, and then you munch.
And as you grind and as you crush,
you mix **saliva** with the mush.

Saliva's filled with enzymes that
begin digesting carbs and fat.
One enzyme working in this space
is starch-digesting **amylase**.

Now, every single starch contains
hundreds of glucoses in chains,
and what the amylase will do
is turn those chains to pairs of two.

(Called "maltose," these are just the prep
for breakdown in a later step,
when maltose will be split again
so only glucoses remain.)

So amylase splits carbs in food
that you've already mushed and chewed.
And now that mushed-up food must go
into the stomach, down below.

In seconds, not too long at all,
the food you're chewing forms a ball:
a mushy **bolus**, soft and round,
that gets pushed back and swallowed down.

It moves into the throat, then must
pass into the **esophagus**.
The bolus makes this tube react
so muscles in its walls contract.

These **peristaltic waves** begin
to push upon the lump within
and slowly move the bolus south
into the stomach's waiting mouth.

(b) The Stomach at Work: Churning and Splitting

The stomach opens just enough
to let in all the swallowed stuff.
It breaks some down, and it may store
the rest for several hours or more.

The stomach's walls are strong; it must
crush foods like chewy pizza crust.
The stomach churns until, in time,
the crust turns into liquid: **chyme**.

All of that chyme gets sloshed around
while enzymes chemically break down
the nutrients, so bit by bit
the **bonds** that make them whole are split.

One enzyme, **lipase**, starts on fat;
another's **pepsin**, something that
breaks proteins. But we're not quite through!
There's still some breakdown left to do.

The stomach's push and grind is slow,
so gradually, the chyme will go
as little squirts of gooey soup
into the small intestine's loop.

(c) The Small Intestine: A Major Role in Breakdown

Inside the small intestine's space,
a lot of final steps take place.
New enzymes split most of the rest
of chyme remaining to digest.

What's left when all this breakdown's through
are **fatty acids**; **sugars**, too;
and also in the mix one finds
amino acids, many kinds.

COOL FACT ABOUT THE STOMACH

- A male **king penguin** can store a whole fish in his stomach for three weeks without digesting it! Our stomachs hold food for only around three hours, and we break down whatever's inside. But the male king penguin is holding that fish for his soon-to-be-hatched chick, so he can't digest it. While his female partner is out fishing at sea, the sacrificing dad cares for his unborn chick: he incubates a single egg on his large flat feet while living off his body fat. Then, if the chick hatches and Mom hasn't returned yet, Dad can chuck up some well-preserved fish to feed his hungry offspring.

COOL FACT ABOUT THE SMALL INTESTINE

- Giraffes have very long small intestines: they can be stretched to reach 180 feet. That's more than half the length of a football field! A cow's small intestine is quite long too; it can stretch to 150 feet. The reason for these extra-long organs is that cows and giraffes are **herbivores**, or plant-eating animals. They need very, very long intestines to help digest and absorb tough **cellulose** in the **cell walls** of the plants they eat. By these standards, the human small intestine is short, at only twenty feet long.

Plus, vitamins like C and A,
and minerals you need each day.
These nutrients are now so small
they'll pass through the intestine's wall.

Now since we've covered quite a lot,
it might seem like we're done; we're not.
It's critical that we discuss
the liver and the pancreas.

(d) The Pancreas and the Liver: Two Organs That Can't Be Left Out

Digesting food does not pass through
these organs, yet they have roles, too.
Assisting food breakdown is one;
then processing when breakdown's done.

First, both these organs will produce
a critical digestive juice.
And then they each deliver this
into your small intestine's mix.

The pancreas produces eight
more enzymes that participate
in the last stages of digestion
of chyme in your small intestine.

The liver's bile is needed too,
as small intestines do not do
too well digesting fat without
a squirt of bile to help them out.

But livers still have work to do
once all of this digestion's through,
because the liver is the thing
that does some final processing.

The nutrients formed by digestion
move out from the small intestine
to the blood, and then they pass
directly through the liver's mass.

The liver stores what cells don't need
right now—but later, it can feed
out nutrients, so that they go
to cells when their supplies get low.

COOL FACTS ABOUT THE LIVER

- In addition to its other functions, the liver also detoxifies blood, turning harmful chemicals into less harmful ones. For example, ammonia, which in large amounts can damage the tissues of the brain, is something we naturally form when **bacteria** break down proteins in the large intestine. Normally, the small amounts we make are picked up in the blood and end up in the liver. The liver turns ammonia into harmless urea, a compound that we easily get rid of in our **urine** and sweat. The liver also breaks down medicines we take so they don't stay in our system for too long.

- Alaskan natives and travelers to the Arctic are often warned to stay away from polar bear livers: eating one can be deadly. The liver stores lots of nutrients for later use, including

some kinds of vitamins, like A, E, and D. Polar bears live in the freezing Arctic, where they don't get to eat vitamin A very often, so they store large amounts of it in their livers. This helps keep them alive, but it's way too much for humans to consume all at once. Though you're not likely to ever eat anything from a polar bear, it's useful to know that we need only tiny amounts of vitamin A every day—too much can be poisonous.

- Most fats don't mix with, or **emulsify**, in water. If you'd like to see this for yourself, try this experiment. Using a jar with a lid, pour in some water and some oil, then shake it up. The oil drops will break up and mix with the water for a little while—this means you've moved the oil around. But since it can't mix permanently with the water, it won't stay put. If you let the mixture sit, the oil will move out of the water and end up on the top, until you shake it up again.

(e) The Large Intestine: Getting Rid of Waste

Digesting food takes lots of time.
Still, we can't break down *all* that chyme;
so wastes remaining from digestion
pass next to the large intestine.

This large organ is the place
where chyme is turned to solid waste.
But it turns out this chyme contains
some nutrients in its remains.

Now, you don't have the enzymes to
break down these last bits coming through.
But luckily there is a fix.
Bacteria take care of this!

We have bacteria that live
in large intestines, and they give
help breaking down wastes to provide
us with the nutrients inside.

Then you make **feces** from the rest:
the parts of food you *can't* digest.
And that's what you eliminate
each time you go to **defecate**.

(f) Summing It Up

So now you've got an overview
of what your pizza must go through
inside that long **digestive tract**.
No pizza bit is left intact.

The next time you eat pizza, just
remember: sauce and fat and crust
transform inside of you to give
you nutrients you need to live!

COOL FACTS ABOUT THE LARGE INTESTINE

- Rabbits eat their own feces. They do this in order to fully digest the cellulose in the plants they feed on. Their large intestines produce two kinds of feces: a soft feces (called "cecotropes"), which are eaten, and later, a hard feces (called "fecal pellets"), which they leave behind.

- Humans are **omnivores**. We eat both plants and meat. We can't, however, digest the tough cellulose walls of plants with our own enzymes; and the bacteria in the large intestine digest only a small amount of the cellulose we eat. So we just eliminate most of the cellulose in our feces.

- There are actually trillions of bacteria that live in the large intestine. And there are thousands of different species! Most of these are helpful bacteria that break down some of the proteins and carbohydrates that our digestive system has been unable to digest on its own. As a result, sugars and important vitamins that we need are released. The good bacteria also help fight off bad bacteria that can make us sick if there are too many of them in our body.

PART II
YUMMY, YUMMY, OR NOT

Why is it certain foods you eat
make your breath smell like stinky feet?
And how can foods your mom likes best
be just the ones that you detest?

Plus, is there any reason why
you can't eat only cake and pie?
How do these foods make us react?
Read on ahead, and learn the facts.

I Really Hate That Broccoli

My older sis loves broccoli,
but it tastes really gross to me.
I take one bite and start to chew,
then spit it out before I'm through.

Mom says it shouldn't be that tough,
but I know when I've had enough.
Please, Dr. Jo, how can it be
that other folks *like* broccoli?

Tell Mom it's **genes** that are to blame
for why our tastes are not the same.
Because of genes, some folks have lots
of **bitter taste receptor** spots,

and it sounds like you're among
those with a bitter-sensing tongue.
But your big sister has so few,
she doesn't taste the way you do.

Another food she'd like, no doubt,
could be a big fat Brussels sprout;
or cabbage, turnips, olives, too.
But these foods might taste sharp to you.

Here's one more option to consider
if you find these veggies bitter:
Roasting sweetens foods a bit.
Or honey might just do the trick.

19

COOL FACTS ABOUT TASTE

- Some prey animals store bitter compounds in their bodies that make them taste disgusting to predators. For example, Australian **cane toads** make many different bitter poisons on the skin that covers their backs. These poisons keep animals like black snakes from eating

them. But the **kite**, a hawklike predatory bird, has a way around this. When a kite catches a cane toad, it just flips the **amphibian** over and eats its fill right from the belly.

- **Monarch butterflies** not only use bitter compounds to avoid getting eaten— they advertise their poison! The colorful butterflies eat milkweed plants when they are **larvae**. These plants contain a bitter chemical that is poisonous to predators but not to the larvae.

The monarch larvae keep the poison in their tissues as they grow, so they become bitter-tasting adults. Adult monarchs advertise their poisons with their bright orange-and-black wings, and most hungry birds stay far away.

- Some people think the herb cilantro tastes like soap! Cilantro, which is commonly used in Mexican and Indian foods, is delicious to many people. But it turns out that certain genes that affect how we smell may also affect our liking of cilantro. Research shows that around one in ten people have the "I hate cilantro" gene.

- You may hate broccoli now but learn to love it when you get older. It's not unusual for the kinds of foods kids like to change when they become adults. At least one reason for this is that children are more sensitive to tastes, especially bitter ones, when they are young. So broccoli that tastes very bitter to you now could taste much less bitter when you are older.

Taste receptors

When I Am Stuffy, Food Tastes Yucky

I have a cold. My nose is stuffed.
It's filled with **mucus**; breathing's tough.
But worst of all, food has no taste:
it's more like cardboard mixed with paste.

Please, Dr. Jo, what's going on?
Just where has all that good taste gone?
I know with colds it's hard to smell,
but why's it hard to taste, as well?

Your **taste receptors** can pick up
sweet, sour, salt, and bitter stuff.
Plus something called **umami**, too:
a meaty taste in soup and stew.

Those taste receptors aren't gone;
when you get stuffed, they still turn on.
The problem is, it's hard to tell
what food you're tasting without smell.

Your food has scents that slowly float
back from your mouth, into the throat,

then up the nose, way deep inside
where tiny **smell receptors** hide.

Inside your nose is really where
we tell an apple from a pear,
or chicken from a piece of fish.
It's smell that makes them taste delish.

But too much mucus blocks the flow;
there's no place for the scents to go.
And without smell, it's hard to savor
food, because you taste less flavor.

If you're stuffy, then you should
find other things that make food good:
like if it's got a spicy kick,
or textures—creamy, thin, or thick,

or if it's chewy, or has crunch.
All that will help you like your lunch.
And soon your cold will end! So then
you'll smell those smells in food again.

MORE COOL FACTS ABOUT TASTE

- Flies can taste with their legs. This makes sense because the first part of the fly that comes into contact with something good to eat is often its legs. For example, if a fly lands on a drop of spilled soda, its legs will detect something sweet, and it can extend its **proboscis** to suck it up. Flies also have **taste buds** on their mouthparts and on the edges of their wings.

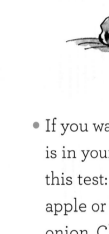

- If you want to see how important smell is in your ability to taste something, try this test: cut up a few small chunks of apple or pear and a few small pieces of onion. Close your eyes and pinch your nose and have someone feed them to you one at a time. You'll be surprised at how hard it is to tell one from the other.

Garlic Gives Me Stinky Breath

It always makes me very mad
when someone says, "Your breath smells bad."
But on my own, I just can't tell
if my breath has a stinky smell.

And here's what gets me even more.
It's garlic from the night *before*
that somehow, slowly, makes its way
into my breath throughout the day!

If I eat mints, or chew some gum,
it's not enough to keep kids from
saying, "Pee-yew, your breath, you reek!"
the minute that I start to speak.

So please do tell me, Dr. Jo,
how garlic breath can somehow grow
from stuff I've eaten yesterday.
And what would make it go away?

It turns out garlic—onions too—
have **sulfur** gases that pass through
your gut, and don't get broken down.
Instead they simply move around.

They get into your blood and seep
out through the lungs, and then they keep
on flowing to your breath, which goes
directly into your friend's nose.

These sulfur compounds are what stay
and make your breath smell bad all day.
So even if a mint is strong,
it won't replace that smell for long.

But it turns out milk binds so well
to sulfurs that they lose their smell.
So garlic bread with milk to drink
will keep you safe; your breath won't stink.

COOL FACTS ABOUT STINKY BREATH

- **Hornworms** use their stinky **nicotine** breath to repel hungry **wolf spiders**. The hornworms, which are the **larval** form of **sphinx moths**, feed on tobacco leaves that are packed with nicotine. It turns out that nicotine is poisonous for many insects, birds, and spiders, but not for hornworms. So hornworms can eat it, store it in their tissues, and become poisonous as well. Then, when they breathe the nicotine out, wolf spiders get the message that these hornworms are dangerous to eat. A few puffs of a hornworm's nicotine-filled breath are enough to make the predator jump back and look for something else to dine on.

- In addition to milk, other foods that help keep away garlic breath are raw apples, spinach, and parsley. All of these foods contain compounds that turn stinky sulfur into other forms that don't stink. They all work best when eaten with the garlicky meal.

- If you still have garlic breath even after eating the right food combinations, don't worry, it will go away eventually. Unfortunately, though, it can take as long as one whole day after you eat the garlic for the stink to disappear!

Why Does Chili Make Me Sweat?

I love my chili spicy, yet
if I eat lots, I start to sweat.
And even if it's cooled a lot,
it still can make my mouth feel hot.

Why does that burn still hang around
in chili that has cooled way down?
I like the heat hot peppers bring,
but do they really have to sting?

The chili that you eat contains
a chemical that can cause pains.
It's called **capsaicin**. It's the thing
that gives your chili heat and zing.

Your mouth and throat have quite a lot
of nerve cells that react to *hot*.
They fire if foods turn out to be
so hot they could cause injury.

These same cells also will begin
to fire if something cuts the skin.
They send a signal to your brain
that makes it sense both heat and pain.

Capsaicin makes nerves fire, but
there is no heat, and there's no cut.
This makes you think that heat is there,
and you can "feel" it everywhere.

It's like capsaicin plays a trick.
The brain's reaction is quite quick:
your throat feels burning all around,
so your brain acts to cool you down.

It sends more blood to your throat's skin,
which should pull heat out from within—
but since there's no real heat in it,
this doesn't help your throat one bit.

The brain may also make you sweat:
sweat normally will cool you. Yet
while your skin cools, your throat will not
feel cooler; it will still feel hot.

So clearly all these things won't treat
your burning throat, since there's no heat.
But you might be surprised to learn
that drinking milk can ease the burn.

'Cause milk has **casein**, which will bind
with the capsaicin, and you'll find
that soon enough your hot cells should
stop all their firing. You'll feel good.

Then you can eat that spicy meal
and never really have to feel
the burn and pain. Now you can boast
that you can eat more *hot* than most!

COOL FACTS ABOUT FOODS
THAT MAKE US FEEL HOT OR COLD

- Humans aren't the only animals that feel a burn from eating chili peppers; squirrels, deer, mice, and most other mammals will not go near the hot stuff. But birds have no problem eating the spicy peppers, because their nerve cells don't respond to capsaicin.

- Scientists believe that peppers evolved to make capsaicin in part to keep seed-digesting mammals from eating them. It turns out that when mammals eat any kind of peppers, their digestive process destroys the small seeds. That would be bad for the plant. Birds, on the other hand, carry the pepper seeds in their guts and then release them with their droppings. This ensures that the chili seeds will be spread around to make new plants.

- Peppermint contains the chemical **menthol**, which acts somewhat like capsaicin, except that it makes us feel cool instead of hot. It stimulates cold receptors, nerve cells that are normally turned on by cold temperatures. It can also stimulate our pain receptors, causing a tingling sensation. Menthol is used in chewing gum, candy, toothpaste, and cough medicines to give our throats a cool feeling, even when we're not cold.

- People often gulp water after eating spicy hot foods. But water doesn't help relieve the burn. Capsaicin is an oily compound that repels water, so water will just spread the chemical around the mouth and make the burn worse. If there's no milk around, try a few spoonfuls of yogurt or sour cream. That should do the trick.

Could I Live on Only Sweets?

Last night I dreamt that I could eat
most every kind of cake and sweet
and lots of cookies, all day long.
So now I wonder: Is that wrong?

Could I just suck on lollipops
or eat red jelly beans nonstop?
It really would be such a treat
to ditch the vegetables and meat.

I'm sorry, but an all-sweets diet
is unhealthy; please don't try it!
You need fats and sugars, sure.
But for good health, you need much more.

You have to get a balanced spread
of vegetables and meat and bread.
Let's take a look at all the things
a healthy, balanced diet brings!

You need the proteins that you gain
when you eat dairy, meat, and grain.
These proteins will be used by cells
to grow, or to replace themselves.

Take skin cells: new ones form each day,
replacing those that flake away.
And muscles, which will grow in size
when you lift weights or exercise.

You need some vitamins, like E
and A and different types of B.
Plus minerals, more than you think,
like iron, calcium, and zinc.

These vitamins and minerals do
a ton of jobs; here are a few.
Your eyes must have some A to see,
and Bs help cells use energy.

There's K for clots that stop a bleed,
and calcium, which all bones need.
We need a bit of zinc as well;
it helps with healing, taste, and smell.

Another mineral we require,
potassium, helps our nerves fire.
Plus blood needs iron that can feed
our cells the **oxygen** they need.

These nutrients have lots to do,
but most don't stay inside of you.
You use them up along the way,
and you must get more every day.

So eat those vegetables and grains,
plus meat and fruit; all these contain
the minerals and vitamins
a healthy person must take in.

Sure, sweets taste great. But here's the deal:
you have to eat a balanced meal.
No matter how your body tries,
it cannot work without supplies.

This body needs fuel!!!

COOL FACT ABOUT SWEETS

- While humans love sweets, cats can't even detect sweetness. Because cats are missing **sweet receptors**, they don't prefer sweet-tasting foods. This makes sense, because in the wild, cats are meat-eating carnivores and don't eat sugars or sugar-producing carbohydrates. But they can detect all the other tastes that you can: sour, bitter, salty, and umami. Another animal that can't taste sweet is the vampire bat, which feeds on protein-rich blood.

PART III
CHOMP, CHOMP, GULP

Why can you gulp saliva down
and still have plenty more around?
How do your swallows usually
move food to where it's meant to be?

Plus, what are things that can disrupt
your swallows, so that drinks squirt up,
or make foods redirect and head
through pathways to the lungs instead?

Let's look at what goes right and wrong
as food gets chewed and moved along.

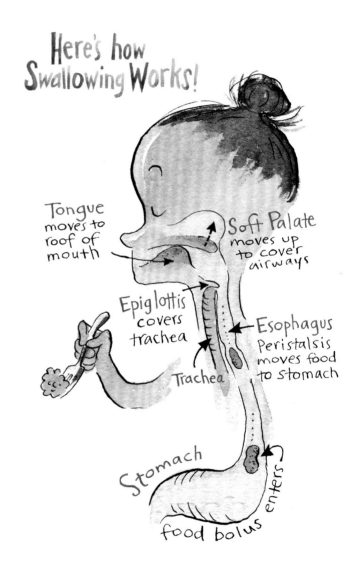

Here's how
Swallowing Works!

Tongue
moves to
roof of
mouth

Soft Palate
moves up
to cover
airways

Epiglottis
covers
trachea

Esophagus
Peristalsis
moves food
to stomach

Trachea

Stomach

food bolus enters

Saliva Never Goes Away

I have saliva night and day.
It never seems to go away.
Each time I eat, I swallow some,
but it's still there when I am done.

I feel saliva everywhere:
below my tongue, a pool's down there;
around my teeth I feel it too;
and yummy smells make more come through.

It seems that there's no end of it.
Why do our mouths make so much spit?
And Dr. Jo, please tell me, too,
what does all that saliva *do*?

Saliva glands, which you can't see,
make new saliva constantly.
You make so much in just one day
it fills four glasses, all the way!

Two cheek **glands** open near your teeth.
Your tongue has four more glands beneath.

All of these glands are what produce
the mix that forms saliva juice.

Your mouth can hold about one cup,
so all the rest gets swallowed up.
And this saliva slowly flows
back to the throat—then down it goes.

So why do you keep making more?
What is all that saliva for?
It might be a surprise to you
to learn how much your spit can do.

One thing saliva does is it
has enzymes that make starches split.
It also kills **germs** that sneak by,
and wets your mouth so it won't dry.

Saliva also makes food paste,
a watery *bolus* you can taste—
'cause it turns out you cannot get
much taste from food unless it's wet.

33

When you need more, there's lots we know
will cause extra saliva flow.
Like if you see a scrumptious treat,
or watch another person eat,

or sniff a real delicious smell,
or taste some food—your senses tell
your brain to send out a command:
"Let's get to work, saliva glands!"

Then right away, there is no wait,
your mouth will start to salivate.
Which means saliva's there to meet
that food you sense *before* you eat.

But even with no food in it,
a healthy mouth still needs some spit.
Your glands produce this juice all day
to keep dryness and germs away.

Now, normally you're not aware
that there's always saliva there.
But if a bug flies in your mouth,
saliva helps you spit it out!

Saliva prevents germs.

gross!

COOL FACTS ABOUT SALIVA

- The six salivary glands are arranged in pairs. They all have big names. The two glands in our cheeks are called the "parotids." The two pairs under the tongue are the submandibulars (which means under the mandible, or lower jaw) and the sublinguals (which means under the tongue).

- Vampire bats have a special chemical in their saliva that keeps a victim's blood flowing. Normally, when you get a small cut, your blood flows for a little while—then in a few minutes your blood makes a small clot, or plug, to stop the flow. But vampire bat saliva has the chemical desmoteplase, or DSPA, that keeps a clot from forming so quickly. So, when the bat makes a small cut in an animal's skin, it has time to suck up enough blood to fill its stomach before a clot forms.

- Small Asian birds called swiftlets build nests made of their own gooey white saliva. The birds use their tongues to deposit drop after drop of saliva on the wall of a cave. The saliva gets hard and forms a clear cup. Here, the swiftlets can lay their eggs and raise their young. Saliva nests are also used in Chinese cooking to make bird's nest soup!

- Without saliva, food wouldn't have much taste. Foods have to be dissolved in saliva to stimulate your taste receptors. You can test this for yourself: first, dry your tongue with a paper towel. Try tasting a dry food like a cracker or pretzel. Then dry your tongue again and try a sprinkle of sugar or salt. Can you taste the food? Now try it with a wet tongue. You should notice a big difference.

My Friend Can Swallow Upside Down

A friend of mine says he has found
that he can swallow upside down.
I'm wondering if this is true,
and could I somehow do it too?

Please, Dr. Jo, this bothers me.
I just don't know how it can be
that if I'm standing on my head,
food won't go down, but up instead.

Yes, you can swallow on your head,
or lying flat upon your bed,
or even while you sleep at night.
The swallow **reflex** gets it right.

Your swallows are amazing things,
'cause normally each gulp will bring
food into the exact right place:
your stomach's empty, waiting space.

A swallow's complicated, though,
cause there are ways food *shouldn't* go.
Like out your lips, so it flies straight
back through the air, onto your plate.

Or to the **trachea**: that's where,
each time we breathe, we take in air.
Food shouldn't go there—it's no joke,
'cause if it does, you'll start to choke.

What's she doing?

Eating lunch.

A third wrong route is one that goes
directly up into the nose.
It does sound gross (but it's quite rare
for swallows to send food up there).

To get it right, a swallow must
close all but the esophagus.
It makes the tongue rise up so that
the ball of food gets pushed on back.

The next step is to quickly close
the pathway leading to your nose,
raising the **uvula**: a flap
that dangles in your mouth, way back.

And last it moves another flap:
the **epiglottis**, which will cap
the trachea. All this will make
a single path for food to take.

Now food can move without much fuss
right into the esophagus.

Once there, your food won't hang around;
the next place it will go is *down*.

But chewed food needs assistance to
squeeze down the tube the whole way through,
cause this food tube is small inside—
it's hardly more than one inch wide.

So the esophageal wall
contracts, and forces food to fall
with peristaltic waves that push
all of the chewed-up, swallowed mush.

These waves ensure that food will go
into your stomach down below.
And if you're standing on your head,
these waves make food go up instead.

But if you laugh or gasp, that may
make swallowed food move the wrong way.
So laugh, then swallow. That is best.
Don't put that reflex to the test!

COOL FACTS ABOUT SWALLOWING

- Sloths always do their swallowing upside down. These large, furry mammals eat while hanging from tree limbs; they will hang upside down for four to six hours a day, munching on leaves. Since all the hanging sloth's organs are above its head, the sloth must swallow everything up instead of down.

- Flamingos also normally swallow up instead of down. These large birds feed by placing their hooked beaks upside down into the mud of a shallow lake. There, they filter out hundreds of tiny organisms called "plankton" from the water. Then they swallow the plankton up their long pink necks and into their stomachs.

- One thing that happens when you swallow is that your tongue moves to the roof of your mouth. Since this is part of a reflex—a process your brain makes occur without your thinking about it—it's very hard to prevent it. Try swallowing some saliva while holding your tongue down on the floor of your mouth. You can do it, but you'll find that it's very difficult.

I'm an antigravity drinking machine!

Talking Sometimes Makes Me Choke

Although I know it's kind of rude,
I like to talk and chew *my* food.
But if I talk too much, I've found,
I start to choke; food won't go down.

So, Dr. Jo, why is it true
that I can't talk and swallow, too?
At other times, it seems as though
my food just *knows* which way to go.

As you now know, your throat's a place
where air and food pass through one space.
And each must be directed to
one of two tubes as it moves through.

The trachea is where air goes
as down into the lungs it flows;
while the esophageal tube
is where we swallow chewed-up food.

To help direct where chewed food goes,
a swallow makes the trachea close.

It does this when a special flap,
the epiglottis, forms a cap.

But if you talk and eat, air might
prevent that flap from closing tight.
And then a bit of food can take
the tracheal pathway by mistake.

A cough or two might be enough
to bring that bit of food back up.
But why take chances? It's no joke.
Don't talk and eat, and you won't choke.

You were saying?

Ack!

39

I Laughed and Milk Came Out My Nose

My friend and I were eating lunch.
I made a joke and laughed a bunch.
And as I laughed, my milk, it rose
up from my mouth and out my nose!

Please, Dr. Jo, why do you think
that laughing made me snort my drink?
I just can't wrap my head around
how my milk could go up, not down.

That's just
sick!

Your nose seems like a little place,
but just behind it, there's more space:
an opening that you can't see.
It's called the **nasal cavity**.

This cavity is where air goes
each time you breathe in through your nose.
Behind this space, your throat connects.
And that is where the air goes next.

But throats transport much more than air,
'cause when you swallow, food goes there.
And both your air and food must be
directed very differently.

This leads to a surprising thing:
you do not breathe while swallowing!
Your swallows take just seconds, then
you very quickly breathe again.

But if you try to drink and laugh,
your milk will travel the wrong path.
'Cause when you laugh, air flows up through
your throat, and moves the milk up too.

The milk gets pushed so that it goes
back toward your head, into your nose.
And then your drink will make its way
out, like a sneeze of snotty spray.

So hold your jokes till eating's done.
Or if you have to tell just one,
and you don't want a nasal burst,
go tell your joke—but swallow first.

COOL FACT ABOUT SWALLOWING AND BREATHING

- Snakes can move their tracheas up out of their mouths when they swallow. This means that they can breathe and swallow at the same time. As you know, people can't do both at once. But for us it's not a problem, since it takes us only a second or two to swallow our food. Snakes, though, often swallow prey bigger than their heads. A python, for example, can swallow an entire deer, or even an alligator! And it takes a very long time to swallow something that big, sometimes more than thirty minutes. So it's important for the snake to be able to keep air coming through while it swallows.

PART IV
GURGLING, GASSY, STOMACH SOUP

Your stomach's quite a noisy place.
So what goes on inside that space?
What makes annoying growls begin,
or causes burps you can't hold in?

And is your stomach overcome
by gluey wads of swallowed gum?
Plus, why does your friend's thrown-up spew
cause you to want to vomit too?

How does your stomach do it all?
Let's take a peek inside its wall.

My Stomach Growls Embarrass Me

When I get hungry, there's no doubt
my empty stomach will send out
loud growls and grumbles, and it's clear
the other kids in class can hear.

I've held my breath, I've really tried,
but I can't stop the noise inside.
So can you tell me, Dr. Jo:
Why does my stomach rumble so?

The stomach growls you heard today
have one odd name that's hard to say.
"BOR-boh-RIG-my" is what's heard.
Borborygmi is the word.

These noises come when stomachs act
to break down food as they contract.
They push and smush the food around
to mash it up and grind it down.

But in the mix is swallowed air
that bubbles through the food in there;

plus, gulps of soda can bring gas
that seeps into the chewed-up mass.

And as your muscles churn and push,
the brew becomes a gassy mush.
This mush, called chyme, gets sloshed around,
and gases make a growling sound.

Then, hours from the time you eat,
your gut contractions will repeat.
Now in the stomach, there's just air,
and it gets pushed around in there.

The gas inside you slowly tumbles,
making more annoying rumbles.
Not lots of noises, just a few.
But other kids might hear them too.

So if those growls embarrass you,
there is one thing that you can do:
eat slowly, because it's been found
that big gulps make more air go down.

COOL FACTS ABOUT STOMACH AND INTESTINAL NOISES

- Stomach growls are loudest when you are hungry because when the stomach is empty, there isn't any partly digested food (or chyme) to absorb the sounds. Hunger growls will normally stop after ten to twenty minutes.

- Even if your gut sounds quiet to you, it can still be making low sounds. A doctor can hear them with a **stethoscope**. You may also hear them in a friend, if you put your ear to his or her belly.

Gulping Soda Makes Me Burp

When I get thirsty, I have found
I like to gulp my soda down.
But then I find I cannot squelch
a really loud, disgusting belch.

I try to hold it in, but then
it quickly pushes out again.
And every time I burp up food,
my mother says, "That's really rude."

So, Dr. Jo, please tell me why,
although I really, really try,
a burp's so very hard to stop.
And could it make my stomach pop?

There's air inside your mouth that you
mix in your food each time you chew.
This means each swallow has a bit
of air that goes along with it.

Plus, bubbles in your soda will
add gas that makes your stomach fill.
But all this extra gas cannot
keep moving down, if there's a lot.

That gas from food or soda pop
can push up on the stomach's top,
and start a reflex, tough to squelch,
that ends up with a great big belch.

The thing this burp reflex will do
is let that extra gas pass through
the throat and mouth: it all comes up
and makes a noisy burp erupt.

And if you try to hold burps in,
your stomach gases can begin
to flow to the intestines, where
some pass as farts into the air.

But please don't fret or think the worst!
You cannot make your stomach burst
by swallowing huge gulps of air.
It all will get moved out of there.

If you'd like to prevent that burp,
it helps if you don't gulp or slurp.
Sip soda slowly. If you do,
your mom will be so proud of you!

Braaaap!

COOL FACTS ABOUT BURPS

- There are valves on either end of the esophagus called the upper and lower esophageal **sphincters**. These sphincters are made of bundles of muscles that circle either end of the tube. The sphincters are normally closed to keep the stomach contents from moving back up to the mouth. But during swallowing, belching, or vomiting, they relax and open up, letting food go down, or gas and digested food come back up.

- A cow normally burps up and farts around eighty gallons of gas every day. That's a lot of gas! Many scientists believe that this "cow gas" plays a role in **global warming**. It results from the work of helpful bacteria in the cow's stomach that break down the cow's grassy meal and release **methane**. Methane is considered a **greenhouse gas**. Greenhouse gases go up into the atmosphere, where they absorb heat, which then warms the earth.

Will Gum I Swallowed Stick Inside?

I was laughing and chewing and swallowed my gum.
And now I'm afraid that I've done something dumb.
I know it sounds silly, but I've got these fears
that the gum will be stuck deep inside me for years.

'Cause gum that I step in sticks right to my shoe,
and I have to scrape hard to get rid of the goo.
So, tell me, please, Dr. Jo, won't that gum stick
to the walls of my stomach? The thought makes me sick.

There's no need to worry, because it's been found
that a chewed piece of gum likely won't stick around.
There's only a small part of gum you digest,
and strong gut contractions remove all the rest.

The parts you digest are the sugars, plus things
like cinnamon, mint, or some fruit flavorings,
and also the oils that make the gum gooey.
But never the **gum base**, the part that's so chewy.

No Worries! It'll all come out in the end!

48

That gum base turns into a small sticky mass.
But your thick stomach muscles will make the wad pass
right through the intestines; these organs are strong.
They can easily push a small gum wad along.

Still, it's likely you don't swallow gum all the time,
so when you need to toss it, please keep this in mind:
throw that gum in the trash can, but wrap it first, too—
or else it might stick to another kid's shoe!

COOL FACTS ABOUT CHEWING GUM

- People have been chewing gum for thousands of years. Even kids in the Stone Age seem to have been gum chewers! Researchers discovered this when they found balls of four-thousand-year-old black tar from birch trees with children's teeth marks in it. Other gum chewers included ancient Greeks, Mayans, and North American Indians, who chomped on different kinds of tree saps. To get the gum, these early chewers made gashes in the trunks of certain trees, then collected the gummy drips of resin and heated them to make them chewy.

- Gum base is the indigestible part of gum. Modern gum bases use mixtures of waxes, rubbers, and latex. Some of these rubbers are also used to make car tires! The rubbers and latexes in gum bases are called **polymers**. These big molecules have a special chemistry that makes them soft and chewy in your warm mouth.

   Once you spit the gum out, though, it gets cold, and its polymers become hard and sticky. That's why gum clings to oils on the surfaces of chairs, sidewalks, and most anything it's put on. Its polymers don't, however, bind to water. This is why you can't just wash away a sticky wad of gum that has been stuck somewhere. Researchers have been working on creating a nonsticky, water-soluble gum—so maybe someday soon you won't have to pull the gooey mess off your shoes or your fingers.

My Friend's Vomit Makes Me Sick

At school today, my friend got sick,
and vomited right on me, ick!
He threw up not just once, but twice.
It smelled so bad; it wasn't nice.

But worst of all, the stuff soaked through
my clothes, and made *me* feel sick too.
I held it in, but I must say,
I felt like throwing up all day.

Why is it *my* friend's vomit will
disgust me so, that *I* feel ill?
One whiff of barf is quite enough
to make me want to heave my stuff.

You vomit to eliminate
bad things you accidentally ate:
bacteria that sometimes hide
in meats that aren't cooked inside,

or nasty germs we know can linger
on a dirty hand or finger.
(They get swallowed when you touch
your fingers to your mouth too much.)

Now, vomiting is the domain
of the **medulla** of the brain.
Medullas control many things,
but two spots are for vomiting.

These "vomit centers" will react
to germs in your digestive tract,
or almost anything at all
that irritates the stomach wall.

So while it feels bad, vomit's good,
because upchucking is what should
remove those germs and poisons, too,
that don't belong inside of you.

Now, sometimes, things that frighten you
can make you want to vomit too.
It's one way for your brain to say,
"That's scary, so get far away!"

Plus, spinning that gets your head reeling
can give you a nauseous feeling,
and gross things you see or smell
can trigger vomiting as well.

The reason someone else's spew
can make you feel so nauseous too,
is this ensures that you won't pick
that nasty food that made *them* sick.

No doubt about it, it's real tough
to be close by when friends throw up.
That stinky vomit's gross, it's true—
but think how it's protecting you!

Mmmmph!!!

Vomiting is good for you!

COOL FACTS ABOUT VOMITING

- **Fulmar** chicks spew out vomit to keep predators away. They can easily shoot a stream of vomit more than six feet, right into the face of an invading crow or hawk. Fulmars are gull-like birds from northern Canada. Adult fulmars can shoot their vomit too, but they don't have the perfect aim of the chicks. That aim is important, since fulmar chicks cannot fly away from predators. A shot of stinky stomach oil is a good way to fight off anything that wants to eat a chick.

- When humans vomit, the walls of the stomach and the esophagus don't contract; they actually relax. It's the walls of the **abdomen**, the part of the body that holds the stomach and intestines, that contract. This contraction pushes on the food in the stomach and upper intestine, forcing it up the esophagus and out through the mouth. Vomiting is a reflex, which means we can't voluntarily control it.

- Cows, sheep, goats, giraffes, and many other hoofed mammals voluntarily move swallowed, partly digested food from the stomach back up the esophagus. This process is called **regurgitation**. It involves contracting special muscles in the wall of the esophagus to force food up instead of down. Animals that do this are called **ruminants**. They eat grasses, shoots, and leaves, which have lots of tough, hard-to-digest cellulose. To break down all their food, ruminants must chew and swallow the food more than once.

  The first time the chewed mass goes down to the stomach, it is mixed with special cellulose-digesting bacteria that start the digestion process. But the bacteria can't get into all of the mass until it's chewed some more. So next, ruminants regurgitate the partly digested food, or **cud**, back up to their mouths. Then they chew and chew and swallow it back down again. Regurgitation is repeated over and over until the food is fully digested.

- What makes you feel like vomiting when you are scared of something, like taking a big test at school or giving a speech in front of the class? The reason is that fear sets off a stress response in your brain called the "fight-or-flight response." This causes your system to release stress hormones that get you ready to fight or run away. Stress hormones affect many parts of your body. Some of the things they do include making your heart beat faster, speeding up breathing, and sending extra blood to the muscles of your legs and brain. At the same time, less blood is sent to your digestive tract. This makes it hard for the stomach and intestines to do their jobs, and they can become irritated. Your irritated digestive tract can make you feel like you want to throw up.

PART V
WHAT A WASTE

So now it's time to finally
learn more about our poop and pee.
Why does poop smell, or come out runny?
Or pee leak when jokes are funny?

Why is it, when farts begin,
it's very hard to hold them in?
Let's take some time to look real close
at things we normally find gross!

I'm Feeling Sick and Have the Runs

I am sick and have the runs,
and I am going tons and tons.
Enough with all the splash and plop!
Please, Dr. Jo, when will this stop?

You caught a bug, or food you ate
brought in some germs that irritate
your stomach, small, or large intestine,
messing with your food digestion.

The process of digestion's slow,
enough to give food time to go
through many different steps, till it's
split up to form small, useful bits.

The stomach uses hours of time
to break food into soupy chyme.
The small intestine is slow too,
with hours of breakdown it must do.

The small intestine sends its waste—
a brown and very soupy paste—
into the large intestine, which
pulls water from the goopy mix.

But germs cause organs to react,
so very quickly, they contract.
This pushes food out much too fast
so that it comes through in a blast,

and there's no time for water to
get pulled out as the wastes pass through.
So your intestine stretches wide
as waste plus water builds inside.

This extra stretch will then create
an urgent need to defecate.
This is a reflex; it's so strong
that you can't hold it in for long.

What comes out is a soupy brew
with undigested food mixed through,
and lots of water in there too.
All this comes pouring out of you.

To replace water, do it right:
get drinks that have **electrolytes,**
like juices, broths, and sports drinks that
will help you get that water back.

As you recover, things will slow,
until you only have to go
just once or twice a day, and you
will feel a whole lot better, too.

It's too far! too far! Oh Noooooo!!!!

COOL FACTS ABOUT DIARRHEA

- **Diarrhea** is a powerful weapon for some animals. With just one squirt, a tiny hoopoe bird chick can stop an invader in its tracks. The antipredator juice is a liquid feces that the little chicks shoot out of their rear ends. A face full of feces is a pretty strong warning to any predator that is thinking of attacking the nest!

- Bird droppings are thick and goopy—more like our diarrhea than the solid chunks we normally defecate. The reason for this is that bird droppings are a mix of both solid wastes and urine. Birds release everything out of one hole, the **cloaca**. So the mix that comes out as a big white splat has both solid and liquid all together. Humans, on the other hand, release these separately: liquid urine comes from our **kidneys** and leaves through a passage called the **urethra,** while solids from our large intestine leave through the **anus**.

Why Can't I Hold My Farts Inside?

I'm so embarrassed when I start
to feel like I'm about to fart.
And when it comes, I might pretend
it's from some other kid's rear end.

Just tell me why, please, Dr. Jo,
I squeeze and squeeze, still out they blow?
And why, as far as I can tell,
sometimes the loudest ones don't smell?

We all pass gases every day,
although it may not seem that way.
Our gas leaks out; it's very slow.
So we don't always feel it go.

Some studies done on farting found
that each of us lets out around
thirteen a day, and with each shot,
there might be odors; there might not.

The big farts that you have to pass
can happen when there's extra gas
inside your colon, which moves fast
out through your anus in a blast.

Now farts, called **flatus**, are a mass
of many different kinds of gas,
including air that's mixed with food
you've swallowed after you have chewed.

What isn't burped can move, intact,
right down through the digestive tract,
on to the large intestine, which
will also add gas to the mix.

'Cause every large intestine holds
bacteria within its folds;
these break down waste that's passing through,
and make more gases when they do.

Those stinky farts you sometimes pass
are from foods that form sulfur gas—
gas your bacteria will make
when they break down remains of steak,

or other foods you might devour,
like broccoli and cauliflower,
plus cabbage, eggs, and onions too.
Still, all these foods are good for you.

And still *more* foods cause gas, it seems,
including apples, pears, and beans,
plus carbs in pasta—bread, as well.
But these form gases that don't smell.

You can't stop flatus, that's a fact.
And you can't hold those big farts back.
But eating slowly will help some:
you gulp less air, less gas will come.

When gas leaves slowly with no smell,
there's no way other folks can tell—
so keep in mind it's not just you.
All of your friends are farting too.

FREEEP!!!

COOL FACTS ABOUT FARTS

- If you really suffer from the smell of your farts, you could try fart-proof underwear! It turns out there are special underpants you can buy made from a carbon material that absorbs fart odors.

- The gases found in flatus are mostly nitrogen, hydrogen, and carbon dioxide. These are the same gases found in air, and they are not smelly. But some folks have certain kinds of bacteria in their large intestines that release small amounts of smelly flatus, containing gases such as **hydrogen sulfide**. Sulfide gases have a strong stink, even in small amounts.

- Everyone farts. Studies have shown that a person typically puts out about one quart of gas each day, on average. These gases pass from us a few ounces at a time, around thirteen times a day. Because most of them come out in small amounts, and most are not smelly, no one notices their passing.

Why Does My Poop Smell So Bad?

When I am pooping, it can make
the bathroom stink—it's hard to take!
And here's another thing I've found:
that awful smell just hangs around.

Plus, I smell other people's poo
in bathroom stalls; it's stinky too.
So, Dr. Jo, what do you think?
What causes all that nasty stink?

Your feces smell because they pass
out of your gut with sulfur gas
made by bacterial digestion
of wastes in your large intestine.

That gas, once it gets out, begins
to float into the air, and then
the air dilutes it. But it's slow;
small bathrooms don't have much airflow.

And that's the reason you have found
the stink of feces hangs around
in bathrooms or in bathroom stalls.
The gases get closed in by walls.

Bacteria might seem quite rude:
they cause that stink, and use your food!
But they make things you need each day,
like vitamins: some Bs and K.

So even though these **microbes** do
make feces stink a lot—pee-yew!—
it's all worthwhile, because they give
you nutrients you need to live.

COOL FACTS ABOUT FECES, AND THE BACTERIA THAT MAKE THEM STINK

- Smelling like poop can be a good thing—at least for the *Hydnora africana*, an African stinking root parasite plant. Its smelly red flowers attract dung-eating beetles with their foul scent. The flower is filled with tiny hairs that trap the beetles inside, so the insects get covered with sticky **pollen**. Then, when the flowers burst open, the pollen-coated beetles can fly off to other stinky root plants and pollinate them. This is how the plants make new seeds.

- The stinkiest gases released from feces are hydrogen sulfides, which smell like rotten eggs, and **methyl mercaptan**, which smells like rotten cabbage.

- It is totally normal to have trillions of bacteria living in your large intestine! Most of the thousands of different species of bacteria there are helpful, but a small number of species are "bad bacteria." These could become harmful if their numbers get too high. Normally, the good bacteria keep the bad ones from multiplying. Helpful bacteria are called **commensal**, because they both get something from us and give something back. What they get from us are foods we cannot digest ourselves, such as cellulose from plants that has made its way down to the large intestine. What we get back from them are nutrients that the bacteria release when they break down the cellulose for energy, and their ability to keep the "bad bacteria" under control.

Why Do I Sometimes Pee So Much?

I'm at the movies with a friend.
It's getting near the very end.
And that is when it comes to me:
I really, really need to pee!

Yet sometimes when I go to play,
and I am out for half the day,
I *never* seem to have to pee.
So, Dr. Jo, how can that be?

Now, you already know the scoop:
digestive waste comes out as poop.
But some digestive waste that's small
does not come out this way at all.

These smaller wastes will slowly go
through organ walls into blood flow.
Then kidneys clean your blood all day
to send these smaller wastes away.

Your kidneys both work constantly
to filter blood and make your pee;
your urine is the way that you
get rid of blood waste passing through.

Your body's needs determine which
things in the blood your kidneys ditch.
Some things you need in small amounts,
but not too much—and that's what counts.

Ahhh...I love science

SALTS
WATER
WASTE
AND...IT'S FILTERED!

Each kidney has a way to track
what's in the blood, and then hold back
things cells might need, if they're too low;
or if they're high, it lets them go.

Like salt: it's needed by each cell,
but with too much, they won't do well.
Plus water: this you clearly need,
but when there's too much, it gets peed.

So, at the movies, you might think
you'll quickly gulp a giant drink.
But one thing you don't think about
is extra soda must come out!

The urge to go comes rapidly
as kidneys turn soda to pee.
This fills your **bladder** up so then
you have to squeeze to hold it in.

Yet on a hot and sunny day,
things may work just the other way.
You run around and sweat and then
lose lots of water through your skin.

So now your kidneys compensate:
they make less urine. You can wait—
you'll run and jump and catch that ball
and never think of pee at all.

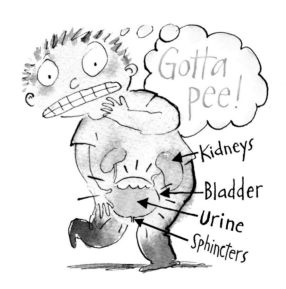

COOL FACTS ABOUT URINE

DON'T shake hands with the monkey!

- **Capuchin monkeys** have a funny way of getting a good grip on things: they engage in a behavior called "urine washing." The monkeys urinate right onto their hands and then rub the smelly liquid on their feet. Any water in the monkey's urine will quickly evaporate, or move from the skin into the air. What's left behind is a sticky, salty mix that helps the monkeys hold on tightly as they climb and jump around in the trees.

- A squirt of urine is a good way for a male porcupine to tell if a female is willing to mate. Since the sharp, spiky quills of a porcupine can be very dangerous, even for another porcupine, it is important for the male suitor to find out if she will allow him to come near. To do this, the male stands on his hind legs and shoots a stream of urine at her. If the female likes the scent of his urine, she'll allow him to come mate with her.

- Male butterflies are often found sipping other animals' urine. The butterflies will gather in groups to drink from a urine-soaked mud puddle. They stick their long proboscises, or mouthparts, into the puddle and sip, often for hours. Other "yummy" fluids butterflies sip from may contain tears, decaying animals, and feces. This behavior is called puddling. It provides the males with salts that they then can give to females during mating. The salts are important for the growth and development of butterfly eggs.

Why Does My Urine Come Out Yellow?

I've noticed, when I go to pee,
the urine that comes out of me
can be dark yellow—or it might
be barely yellow. Is this right?

Oh, Dr. Jo, it seems so strange
to have my urine's color change!
And why is it that normally
there's yellow color in my pee?

It turns out **urochrome**'s the thing
inside your urine that will bring
a yellow color to your pee.
The more there is, the more you'll see.

Now, urochrome is what comes round
as livers break old red cells down.
What red cells spew, when they are dead,
is **hemoglobin**, which is red.

Old hemoglobin will get changed
as all its parts are rearranged,
so that some urochrome is made.
This compound has a yellow shade.

This yellow urochrome won't stay;
the liver's blood sweeps it away
off to the kidneys, which then take
it to the urine that they make.

While urochrome makes yellow pee,
your normal urine's going to be
mixed in with lots of water, too.
This gives it a light yellow **hue**.

But if you start to sweat a lot,
your kidneys make sure you will not
release much water; then you'll find
your urine's the deep yellow kind.

So when you're sweaty, normally
you'll make a darker yellow pee.
And when you're not, more water goes
out, so a paler yellow shows.

What all those different yellows show
is kidneys can change urine flow
based on your body's needs, and fix
the water content in the mix.

It's so amazing when you think
that what you sweat or what you drink
affects the water in your pee
and how much yellow you will see!

MORE COOL FACTS ABOUT URINE

- Eating asparagus can make urine smell like boiled cabbage! But only some people make asparagus urine, and only some people can smell it. The ability to make asparagus urine and the ability to smell it are caused by each person's unique genetic makeup. The stinky odor comes from sulfur chemicals in the asparagus, which are similar to the chemicals that make farts stinky.

- Rabbits and deer have been observed to leave tracks of blue urine in the snow. This is because the animals eat buckthorn, a shrub with dark purple berries. Rabbits occasionally munch the bark and twigs of the buckthorn, and deer eat the berries. A chemical in these plants gives the animals a dark yellow urine, which turns blue after being exposed to sunlight.

- Some people produce pink or red urine after eating beets. This condition is called "beeturia," and it is totally harmless. Beeturia occurs in only about one out of ten people. People with this condition have trouble digesting the chemical betalain, which makes beets pink. This means that the betalain will stay in the blood and eventually come out in the urine.

- If you want to see how the amount of water in your urine affects how yellow it is, try this simple experiment. Take a half glass of orange juice. Add a little water to it. Notice how the color gets paler. Add more and it will get even paler. By adding the water, we're making the juice more dilute and lighter in color. Orange juice without much water in it, on the other hand, is a **concentrate** and will look dark in color. The same is true for your urine.

I Laughed So Hard It Made Me Pee

This really, really bothers me:
sometimes I laugh so hard I pee.
And then I need to do a dance
to keep what's left inside my pants!

So, please do tell me, Dr. Jo,
why laughing makes me have to go—
though right before, as I recall,
I had no need to pee at all.

Most of the time, you can control
the urine that your bladder holds,
'cause at its exit, there are two
round sphincters guarding what gets through.

These rings of muscle stay shut till
the bladder really starts to fill.
Its stretching walls send signals that
will tell the brain, "It's time to act."

This makes one sphincter open wide
to let out all the pee inside.
The muscled bladder contracts too,
to help to push that urine through.

But nothing comes out until you
decide to open number two.
So you can hold it closed and wait
for the right time to urinate.

But once you let that sphincter go,
your urine quickly starts to flow.
And when you're laughing, it can be
extremely hard to hold your pee.

The problem is the laughing act.
It causes muscles to contract
around your **chest** and abdomen,
which push your bladder, pressing in.

This pressure can be just enough
to open *both* the sphincters up,
which makes it very hard to keep
your urine in—and you might leak.

So even though you're thinking, *Please
don't let me pee!* and try to squeeze,
or even if you do a dance,
there's still a chance you'll pee your pants!

COOL FACT ABOUT URINATION

- A person, a little dog, and a big elephant all take almost the exact same amount of time to urinate: around twenty-one seconds. This may seem strange when you think about the fact that an elephant is releasing more than twenty-six gallons in one shot, while a person or a dog releases only a few cups. Gravity from the weight of all that heavy liquid helps elephants' urine shoot out in a powerful jet. On the other hand, smaller animals like dogs, cats, and people, with much less urine to release, produce a slow, steady stream.

CONCLUSION
SOME FINAL THOUGHTS

At last, we're finally at the end.
We've covered every curve and bend
of the digestive tract for you,
and traced the path of food straight through.

And we made sure not to leave out
some topics you're concerned about,
like vomit, stinky poop, and farts.
They're gross, but still, they play their parts!

So what digestion's all about
is taking food and pulling out
nutritious things that get sent to
each hungry cell inside of you.

At the same time, this system's good
at moving out the things that should
be gotten rid of rather fast:
like nasty bugs, food wastes, and gas.

In all, it's quite amazing that
the carbs, the proteins, and the fat
we eat will be transformed to give
us everything we need to live.

Still, we should really think about
what we take in and what comes out;
digestive tracts love balanced meals.
Eat well—you'll see how good it feels!

GLOSSARY

Abdomen: The area of the body under the rib cage and the large, flat breathing muscle called the diaphragm. The abdomen houses many organs, including the stomach, liver, pancreas, small intestine, large intestine, kidneys, spleen, and urinary bladder.

Absorb: To take in or suck something up. After we digest our food, the nutritious molecules that are left are absorbed by the stomach, small intestine, and large intestine when they move across the walls of these organs and into the blood.

Amino acids: These are the building blocks of proteins. When a protein is digested, it is broken down into many different amino acids. There are twenty different kinds of amino acids, and nine of them—including histidine, valine, isoleucine, leucine, phenylalanine, threonine, tryptophan, methionine, and lysine—must come from our diet. Amino acids from our food are absorbed into the blood and carried to the liver, which uses them to make new proteins that the body needs.

Amphibian: Amphibians are four-footed animals that include frogs, toads, and salamanders. They have backbones and so are considered vertebrates. Most amphibians spend part of their lives on land and part in water. They are also ectotherms, meaning they can't regulate their own body heat from the inside. Instead, they use sunlight and burrows for warmth and shade, and water to cool down.

Amylase (salivary amylase): Amylases are a group of similar enzymes that break down starch into sugars. They are found in saliva and in the digestive juices that the pancreas releases into the small intestine.

Anus: The opening at the end of the large intestine. Feces move out through the anus when they leave the body.

Atoms: Atoms are the very tiny building blocks of all things. They are so small you can only see them with a special microscope. Atoms link together to form molecules like carbohydrates, proteins, and fats. Your whole body, with all its different molecules, contains billions of atoms.

Bacteria: Tiny living organisms that can be seen only under the microscope. Some bacteria are responsible for causing infections like strep throat and some types of pink eye. Others live in our digestive tract and help us digest food. These "good" bacteria help to fight off the bad ones.

Bile: Bile is a substance that helps us digest fat. Bile mixes with large droplets of fat and breaks them into small ones. Bile is made in the liver and stored in a pouch called the gall bladder. It then travels through special ducts to the intestine, where it can do its work.

Bind: When things bind to each other, they become attached or stuck together. For example, proteins bind cells together to form tissues.

Bitter taste receptors: Taste receptors that detect bitter flavors, like unsweetened chocolate, black coffee, olives, and Brussels sprouts. Some people are more sensitive to bitter tastes than others. These folks might prefer sweeter versions of chocolate or coffee.

Bladder (urinary): A muscular sack that receives urine from the kidneys and holds it until there is enough to trigger urination.

Bolus: A round, soft mass of partly digested food. After food is chewed and mixed with saliva in the mouth, it is called a bolus. The bolus is swallowed into the esophagus on its way to the stomach.

Bonds: Molecules like proteins, fats, and carbohydrates are made up of smaller molecules, which are held together by chemical connections, or bonds. When we digest the big molecules, we break some of their bonds to form the smaller ones. Small molecules can move through the walls of the stomach, small intestine, and large intestine to be absorbed into the blood.

Borborygmi (pronounced BOR-boh-RIG-my): Growls or rumbles in the stomach, small intestine, and large intestine. These sounds are made when the stomach and intestines contract, causing food, liquids, and swallowed gases to move around inside them.

Building blocks: Molecules like proteins, fats, and carbohydrates are built from smaller molecules. These smaller molecules are called building blocks. The building blocks of proteins are amino acids; the building blocks of fats are glycerol and fatty acids; the building blocks of carbohydrates are simple sugars like glucose, fructose, and galactose.

Calories: Calories are units of energy. The food molecules we eat have energy inside them. When we break down these molecules, their energy is released for our bodies to use. When we eat more calories than our bodies can use right away, the extras are stored as fat.

Cane toad: A large toad that has poison glands on its skin. A cane toad's poison is dangerous to most animals that try to eat it. Cane toads can reach half a foot long, and they are found in Central and South America, as well as the Caribbean islands and Australia.

Capsaicin: A chemical found in chili peppers that makes them taste hot.

Capuchin monkeys: Long-tailed brown monkeys with tan or white faces. Capuchins spend most of their time swinging through trees hunting for fruit, leaves, insects, small birds, and frogs to eat. They are found in South and Central America.

Carbohydrates (carbs): Carbohydrate molecules are built from the atoms carbon, oxygen, and hydrogen and are found in all kinds of foods. Different types of carbohydrates include sugars (like glucose, sucrose, lactose, and fructose), starches, and cellulose. Sugars are found in almost everything we eat, including milk, cereals, fruits, breads, and cake. Starch is found in foods like bread, potatoes, cereals, pasta, rice, and beans. Cellulose is found in plant cell walls and is something we can't digest without help; bacteria in our large intestine break down some of it, and we eliminate the rest in our feces.

Casein: A protein found in milk and other dairy products that can lessen the burn that comes from the capsaicin in chili peppers. Casein does this by binding, or attaching, to capsaicin so the hot chemical can't stimulate pain receptors in the mouth.

Cell walls: The thick outer coverings of plant cells, and cells from some other organisms like bacteria. Cell walls are made of cellulose, a tough fiber. Animal cells lack a cell wall and have only a thin cell membrane instead.

Cells: The basic building-block unit of all living things. Every part of the body is made up of cells, which combine to form tissues. Tissues then combine to form organs like the stomach and kidneys and brain. There are many different kinds of cells in the body, each with its own function. Some examples include cells that protect parts of the body (skin cells), release wastes (kidney cells), move body parts (muscle cells), support the body (bone cells), and think (brain cells).

Cellulose: A tough carbohydrate made up of a chain of glucose molecules. Cellulose is found in cell walls. Humans lack the enzymes to digest cellulose, but it forms part of the fiber that we need to move food easily through the digestive tract. Animals that live on plants, like horses, cows, and rabbits, have large numbers of cellulose-digesting bacteria in their guts that help break down nearly all the cellulose to release its nutrients.

Chemistry: The science that deals with the makeup of substances, and how they change and interact with other substances. So, for example, the chemistry of glucose tells us that it is made up of carbon, hydrogen, and oxygen atoms. It also tells us that glucose molecules can link with each other in chains to build other carbohydrates, and that they can be broken down in cells to release energy.

Chest: Also known as the thorax, the chest is the region of the body surrounded by the rib cage. Inside it are the heart, lungs, trachea, and esophagus. The chest is separated from the lower part of your body, the abdomen, by a flat breathing muscle called the diaphragm.

Chyme: The watery mass that forms after food is digested in the stomach. It is this mass that then moves on to the small intestine. When we vomit, we bring up chyme.

Cloaca: An opening found in birds that is used both for release of any wastes and for reproductive purposes. Both urine and feces are released through the cloaca.

Commensalism (commensal): When two organisms live together and both benefit from the relationship. For example, we have a commensal relationship with the helpful bacteria that live in our large intestine. We benefit because the bacteria break down certain proteins found in our wastes, releasing nutrients to us. The bacteria benefit from us by using some of the energy they release for their own survival.

Compounds: A chemical compound is a substance built from two or more different atoms. Carbon dioxide is a compound made up of one carbon atom and two oxygen atoms.

Concentrate: A mixture in which most of the water or other liquid has been removed, so what's left behind is thicker and takes up less space.

Contractions (contract): When the fibers inside a muscle move together to do work, you say that the muscle is contracting. This means it produces something called force, a power that can be used to hold up the body, move body parts, or move things inside the body. A contracting muscle can pull on bones to move them, or hold up things like the head. During digestion, muscles inside the digestive tract contract to push food and waste through and to break food down.

Cud: Partly digested food from the stomachs of animals like cows, goats, and giraffes. After it is first swallowed, food is partly digested by stomach bacteria and then sent back up to the mouth for more chewing. When this food, now called cud, is finally swallowed back to the stomach, it is well broken down and ready for final digestion.

Defecate: To release feces from the body.

Diarrhea: Feces that come out thin and watery.

Digestive tract: Also called the "GI (gastrointestinal) tract," this passage in our body is made up of the hollow organs that food passes through when we digest it. These organs include the mouth, esophagus, stomach, small intestine, and large intestine.

Electrolytes: Substances that mix in with, or dissolve, in water to create a solution that has an electrical charge. Electrolytes are found in the blood, the fluids of our cells, and the fluids that surround the cells. They are needed by cells for all kinds of everyday functions, like making nerve cells fire and muscles contract. They also help move nutrients, like sugars; wastes; and gases, like oxygen, into and out of our cells. In the body, common electrolytes include sodium, potassium, and chloride. Our kidneys help balance the electrolytes in our body fluids.

Emulsify: To emulsify is to mix together two liquids that don't normally mix. The fats we digest come into the small intestine as large globs that won't mix with lipases, the fat-digesting enzymes in watery intestinal juices. So chemical bile is needed to emulsify the fat, breaking it up into tiny droplets that mix around with the lipase. The lipase can then bind to the little droplets and digest them.

Energy: Power that makes things move or change. The body needs energy for everything it does. Molecules hold energy in their bonds. Our cells normally get energy by breaking the bonds between the carbon, hydrogen, and oxygen atoms in glucose and fats.

Enzymes: Chemicals that speed up chemical changes or reactions. There are different enzymes for each chemical reaction in the body. For example, the starch you get in a bite of bread splits into smaller sugar molecules when mixed with the enzyme amylase.

Epiglottal flap (epiglottis): A flap of hard tissue (called "cartilage") in the throat that forms a cap, which covers the trachea when swallowing. This cap directs swallowed food into the esophagus and down toward the stomach. It ensures that food does not go into the trachea and lungs.

Esophagus (esophageal tube): A muscular tube that runs from the throat to the stomach. When we swallow, food passes into the esophagus.

Extract: To pull something out of something else. During digestion, we extract nutrients from the food we eat and get rid of what's left as wastes.

Fat: A nutrient found in most of the food we eat. There are many kinds of fats, but all of them are built from fatty acids and glycerol molecules. Cells can use these molecules for energy, to build new cells, and to make some important hormones.

Fatty acids: Fatty acids are molecules that form parts of fats. They are built from chains of carbon, hydrogen, and oxygen atoms. When we break down fats, we release fatty acids. Fatty acids are important molecules that our cells can use for energy.

Feces: Wastes formed in the large intestine from the parts of foods that we don't digest.

Flatus: Flatus is gas that is produced in the stomach and both intestines during digestion. It is released through the anus as a fart.

Fuel: Fuel is something that is broken down to get energy. Our cars get energy when they break down gasoline. Our cells get energy by breaking down sugars, fatty acids, and occasionally other nutrients. When they do this, we say they "burn fuel." This does not mean that there is a fire in the cells; only that the cells are breaking down nutrients, releasing heat and energy.

Fulmars: These are seabirds that look like gulls with larger beaks. They feed on fish and other seafood and spend most of their lives at sea. Fulmars come to land to breed. Their chicks protect themselves from predators by vomiting an oily gastric juice at them.

Genes: Genes are a critical part of what determines everything about us: things like the color of our eyes, the shape of our nose, and how tall we grow. Genes are found in all of our cells, and they come from our parents—we say they are "inherited" from our parents.

Germs: Living things, or organisms, that make us sick. Germs include harmful or "bad" bacteria, viruses, and fungi.

Glands: Organs in the body that make and release substances that we need, like digestive enzymes, hormones, sweat, and oils.

Global warming: Global warming is the slow warming of the earth's surface, atmosphere, and oceans. Scientists believe that one cause of global warming is high levels of greenhouse gases, like carbon dioxide—which forms when we burn fuel like coal, oil, and gasoline—and methane from cows. Here's how it works. Normally, when the sun's rays hit the earth, they warm it. The earth then sends a portion of these heat waves, slightly changed, back into the atmosphere. This keeps the earth warm, but not too warm. But when extra greenhouse gases move into the atmosphere, they can sit there above the earth, blocking some of these heat waves from getting out. So the heat waves stay on the earth, making it warmer than normal.

Glucose: A sugar that is the main molecule that our cells break down for energy.

Greenhouse gases: Gases in our atmosphere that trap heat. By keeping heat close to the earth, these gases are thought to contribute to global warming.

Gum base: Gum base is what makes gum chewy. In the past, gum base was made from chicle, the sap of the Central American sapodilla tree. This sap is a mix of chemicals that can be used to make rubber. Today, a man-made rubber is usually used instead. The rubbery gum base is chewy, but not digestible, so it passes harmlessly through the digestive tract if it is swallowed. Gums also have flavorings, sweeteners, and oils to make them soft; these parts *are* digested.

Hemoglobin: Hemoglobin is a molecule in our red blood cells that carries oxygen. Hemoglobin molecules pick up oxygen in the lungs and carry it throughout the body, releasing it to hungry cells. When hemoglobin has oxygen attached, it turns bright red in color. This is what makes our blood red.

Herbivores: Herbivores are animals that feed on only plants. They include horses, cows, goats, sheep, rabbits, and many others.

Hormones: Chemicals that help the body with hundreds of different day-to-day functions. Hormones help cells take in nutrients, make bones grow taller, make the heart beat faster when we're running, and make male or female sexual parts grow and develop. Hormones are released into the blood and carried to cells, where they do their jobs. Some hormones involved in digestion include the hormone insulin, which helps our cells absorb sugar from the blood; the hormone gastrin, which stimulates the stomach to release digestive juices when food is present; and the hormone ghrelin, which makes us feel hungry when the stomach is empty.

Hornworms: A type of green caterpillar that eventually turns into a large brown sphinx moth. The hornworm feeds on the leaves and fruits of tomatoes and tobacco plants. Eating tobacco leaves gives hornworms a stinky breath that keeps predators away.

Hue: A hue is a shade of a color. A lemon could be described as having a bright yellow hue. The sky has a light blue hue.

Hydrogen sulfide: A gas with an odor like rotten eggs. It contains atoms of hydrogen and sulfur.

This stinky gas is common in swamps, volcanoes, and sewers, and it's made in small amounts by bacteria in the large intestine. It is one of the gases that gives feces their stinky odor.

Intestine: A part of the digestive system that runs between the end of the stomach and the anus. It is a coiled tube that is divided into a thin, long small intestine and thicker large intestine.

Kidneys: Organs that filter wastes from the blood and create urine. Wastes can be anything that the blood has too much of, including water, salts, acids, and urea, which we make when we break down amino acids in the body.

King penguin: A very large penguin that can grow to three feet in height and weigh up to thirty-five pounds. Like all penguins, it is a flightless bird. It feeds in the Southern Ocean and lives near the cold waters north of Antarctica, in very large colonies of up to 450,000 birds.

Kites: Birds of prey related to eagles. Kites are large, soaring birds with hooked beaks. They feed in daylight, diving from the sky to capture amphibians like cane toads, as well as small birds, mice, reptiles, and fish.

Large intestine: The second part of our intestine. It is around five feet long in adults and is where wastes are turned into feces. There is absorption here of water and some remaining nutrients.

Larvae, larval: Larvae are young animals that will later change into different adult forms. This change is known as metamorphosis. Insects, fish, and amphibians all have larval stages. In butterflies, the larval form is a caterpillar. In frogs, it is a tadpole.

Lipase: An enzyme that speeds up the breakdown of fats into fatty acids and glycerol.

Liver: A large organ with many critical digestive functions. The liver absorbs the small molecules that are formed during digestive breakdown of large molecules like glucose, fructose, fatty acids, and amino acids. It can then rebuild these products into different carbohydrates, fats, and proteins that the body needs. The liver also stores sugars and fats for later use, and manufactures bile.

Medulla: A part of the brain that keeps our heart beating at the right rate and keeps our lungs breathing. In digestion, it controls swallowing. The medulla's functions are involuntary: they happen without our having to think about them.

Menthol: A chemical from mint plants that makes the skin or mouth feel cool. It works by binding, or attaching, itself to cold receptors in the skin or throat. Cold receptors are nerve cells found in places like the skin and mouth that will fire when the temperature around them drops, telling the brain that you are cold. Your cold receptors fire in response to menthol just like they would if the air was cold; so you have a sense of feeling cool even though you aren't.

Methane: A gas released into the air from burning fuel, burping cows, and bacterial breakdown of garbage in landfills or garbage dumps. Methane traps heat in the air and plays an important part in warming the earth (see global warming).

Methyl mercaptan: A gas with the odor of rotten cabbage. It is found in foods like onions, garlic, meat, and eggs. Small amounts are also found in our blood and brains. It mixes in with our feces and is part of what gives feces their smell.

Microbe: A living thing that is so small, you can only see it with a microscope. Microbes include organisms like bacteria and viruses (although not all scientists agree that viruses are living things). Microbes can be harmful—like disease-causing bacteria—or helpful, like some of the bacteria in our digestive tract that help break down our food.

Micturition reflex: The reflex involved in urination. When the bladder fills with urine, it stretches. This stimulates the reflex, which makes muscles in the wall of the bladder contract and squeeze on the urine inside. At the same time, it also makes one of the sphincters guarding the opening to the urethra relax, so we need to urinate. If the need isn't too strong, we can control urination by holding closed a second sphincter around the urethra until we are ready to go.

Minerals: A type of nutrient that the body needs to work normally. Important minerals for our bodies include calcium, iron, magnesium, phosphorus, potassium, sulfur, chlorine, sodium, zinc, copper, manganese, and selenium. Minerals have a wide range of functions, including building bones, forming blood and hormones, and playing a role in muscle contraction.

Molecule: A molecule is a chemical made of two or more atoms that are linked together. The atoms can be the same or different. For example, glucose is a sugar molecule that is made up of six carbon atoms, six oxygen atoms, and twelve hydrogen atoms. Molecules are very, very small and can only be seen with a special microscope.

Monarch butterfly: A large orange-and-black butterfly that predators avoid because it is poisonous to eat. Monarchs get their poisons from feeding on milkweed plants when they are in the caterpillar stage. They store the toxic milkweed juices in their tissues, which makes them taste terrible to predators.

Mucus: A thick, slippery liquid that keeps our body passageways moist. Mucus is produced by glands in the linings of the digestive, urinary, and respiratory tracts.

Nasal cavity: The space in the skull behind the nose. When we breathe, air moves in through the nose and then into the nasal cavity on its way to the throat.

Nerves (nerve cells): Nerves are bundles of nerve cells, or neurons. Individual neurons carry messages to or from the brain or from one part of the brain to the other. There are different types of neurons. Sensory neurons take messages to the brain from sense organs involved in sight, hearing, taste, smell, and touch. Motor neurons take messages from the brain, telling your muscles to contract to move your limbs or your digestive organs. For example, when your tongue pushes a bolus of chewed food to the back of your mouth, sensory neurons in the mouth (called touch receptors) detect it and take a message to the brain that there is food to be swallowed. Motor neurons from the brain then send a message to the muscles in the tongue, soft palate, and throat, setting off the swallowing reflex.

Nicotine: A chemical found in cigarette tobacco. When people smoke cigarettes, nicotine enters the blood and gets carried to the brain. While nicotine briefly stimulates the brain, it also increases the heart rate, breathing rate, and blood pressure. Nicotine makes cigarettes extremely addictive, which means that once you start smoking, it's very hard to stop doing it. Long-term cigarette smoking has been found to increase the risk of heart disease and cancer.

Nutrients: Chemicals in foods that our bodies use for energy, cell building, and all kinds of body functions. Proteins, carbohydrates, fats, water, minerals, and vitamins are all types of nutrients.

Omnivores: Omnivores are animals that eat both plants and other animals. Humans are omnivores. Other omnivores include bears, pigs, raccoons, mice, ants, and flies.

Organs: Parts of the body with specific functions, or jobs to do. Each organ is made up of two or more tissues. The digestive organs include the mouth, esophagus, small intestine, large intestine, liver, gall bladder, and pancreas.

Oxygen: A gas in the air we breathe. Our cells need oxygen to break down glucose for energy. Cells also use oxygen to build new molecules from the food we digest. Oxygen-containing molecules include carbohydrates, fats, and proteins. These molecules are then used to make new cells, create enzymes, and do many other everyday tasks.

Pancreas: An organ that has two different kinds of digestive functions. One is to make digestive enzymes. The other is to make the hormones insulin and glucagon, which work to move glucose into or out of the blood based on the needs of the body.

Pepsin: A stomach enzyme that aids in the breakdown of proteins. It is released into the stomach in an inactive, or nonworking, form, and is activated by stomach acids.

Peristaltic waves (peristalsis): Waves of muscle contraction that push food through the digestive tract. They occur in the esophagus, stomach, and small and large intestines.

Pollen: Tiny grains made by plants when they reproduce. Pollen grains are actually sperm cells. They are made by the male parts of a plant, the stamens, and they combine with eggs made by the female part of the plant, the pistils, to produce seeds.

Polymers: Large molecules built from smaller building-block molecules that repeat over and over again. Starch is a polymer made up of many, many glucose molecules linked together in chains. Other polymers include the rubbers and latexes that are found in chewing gum.

Proboscis: A long, skinny tube that acts as the mouth for some insects. Butterflies use their proboscises to suck nectar from a flower, or salty urine from the ground.

Proteins: Large molecules that are built from chains of amino acids. Proteins we eat are used to build new cells, and to create enzymes and some hormones.

Red blood cells: Microscopic round cells in the blood, which carry oxygen from the lungs to all the tissues of the body.

Reflex: The body's response to a particular stimulus that happens automatically, or without your having to think about it. For example, after food has been chewed in the mouth, the bolus pushes on the back of the mouth, automatically triggering the swallowing reflex.

Regulate: To regulate means to control something. Both your nervous system and your hormones regulate all the different things that happen during digestion. For example, when food enters the stomach, some of the chemicals in the food stimulate the release of the hormone gastrin. Gastrin regulates the stomach: it causes it to release digestive juices and to contract, grinding up food and pushing it toward the small intestine.

Regurgitation (regurgitate): The flow of the stomach contents up into the mouth. It is sometimes used as a synonym for vomiting. While most humans have no control over regurgitation, some animals can do it voluntarily. Cows, giraffes, and other cud chewers regurgitate partly digested food so they can re-chew and redigest it. Penguins and some other birds regurgitate food into their mouths to feed their chicks.

Ruminant: An animal that chews its cud. Ruminants feed on grass and other plants that are difficult to digest. After breaking down the food in one region of the stomach, these animals regurgitate partly digested food, or cud, back into their mouths. Here, it is re-chewed and swallowed and then passed to another part of the stomach for further digestion. Ruminants include cows, goats, sheep, deer, giraffes, and camels.

Saliva: Saliva is a digestive juice that is made in the mouth by the salivary glands. It is almost 99 percent water, but it also has the enzyme salivary amylase, which begins starch digestion, and mucus, which helps us swallow. In addition, it has bacteria-killing lysozymes and many different kinds of salt.

Saliva glands (salivary glands): Three pairs of glands in the mouth that produce saliva. They are the parotids, the sublinguals, and the submandibular glands.

Small intestine: The first part of our intestine. It stretches to about twenty feet in adults. It is the place where a lot of chemical breakdown and absorption of digested food and water takes place.

Smell receptors: Nerve cells designed to pick up odors. Millions of smell (or olfactory) receptor cells cluster together in the upper part of the nasal cavity. Humans can detect over a trillion different odors with these cells.

Soft palate: The soft tissue that forms the back part of the roof of the mouth. The front part of the roof is called the hard palate. On top of the hard and soft palate is the nasal cavity. When we swallow, muscles inside the soft palate contract and move it up so it will block the opening to the nasal cavity, and swallowed food won't go out the nose.

Sphincters: Rings of muscle that guard many of the entries and exits to the organs of the digestive tract. When these muscles squeeze, or contract, the passage they guard closes. When the muscles relax, the passage opens, and partly digested food or wastes can move to the next organ or out of the body. For example, there is an upper esophageal sphincter guarding the entrance to the esophagus from the throat. There

is also a lower esophageal sphincter guarding the exit from the esophagus to the stomach. Other sphincters include the internal and external sphincters at the exits of the urinary bladder and the anus of the large intestine, which control the release of urine and feces, respectively.

Sphinx moths: Large, fast-flying moths that hover over flowers like hummingbirds. Their larval form is the fat green hornworm caterpillar, which loves to dine on tobacco leaves and garden vegetables like tomatoes.

Starch: A carbohydrate found in foods like bread, pasta, rice, corn, potatoes, fruit, and seeds. It is made up of chains of glucose molecules. In digestion, starch is eventually broken down into many molecules of glucose, which our cells use for energy.

Stethoscope: A tool used by doctors to listen to the heartbeat and other body sounds. It has a rubber tube with a small round metal disc at one end. The disc makes the body sounds louder to the ear of the listener. On the other end, the tube splits into two branches, with earpieces on either side.

Stomach: A stretchy sac that runs from the end of the esophagus to the beginning of the intestines. The stomach plays a role in breaking down food through the churning of its thick, muscular walls. It also releases juices (acid and enzymes) that are important in the chemical breakdown of certain foods. Water and some digested foods are absorbed through the stomach walls.

Sugars: Small carbohydrate molecules that dissolve in water and make things taste sweet. Sugar molecules are all made up of carbon,

hydrogen, and oxygen, arranged in different ways. Some types of sugars that are found in our foods include glucose, sucrose, lactose, and maltose.

Sulfur: A bright yellow element that combines with other elements to form stinky compounds. One of these is hydrogen sulfide, which is a gas that makes rotten eggs smell rotten. It's also one of the things that makes farts and feces stinky.

Sweet receptors: Nerve cells that detect sugars, and some other molecules that we sense as sweet. They are found on the tongue.

Taste buds: Small clusters of taste cells, or taste receptors. Most of our ten thousand taste buds are on the top of the tongue. We also have some inside our cheeks, on our soft palate, and in our throat.

Taste receptors: Sensory cells that detect tastes and are found in our taste buds. We have five known kinds of taste receptors: for the tastes sweet, sour, salty, bitter, and umami. Taste scientists are currently doing research to search for other kinds of receptors.

Tissue: A tissue is a group of cells that work together to do a job in the body. One type of tissue in the digestive tract is the epithelial tissue that lines the inside of the digestive organs and produces mucus and digestive enzymes. Another example is the muscle tissue inside the walls of the digestive organs, which contracts to move and break down food.

Trachea (windpipe): A tube that carries air from the throat to the lungs. It runs through the neck, in front of the esophagus. When we swallow, the epiglottal flap closes off the opening to the trachea so food can only go down the esophagus.

Umami: A type of taste described as meaty or savory. It makes many meats and cheeses tasty. Umami receptors are one of the five known kinds of taste receptors in our mouths.

Urethra: A tube that carries urine from the urinary bladder out of the body. In males, the urethra runs through the penis, and also carries sperm.

Urine (urinate): A yellow, liquid waste, also called pee, that is formed in the kidneys and released from the urinary bladder. To urinate is to release urine from the body.

Urochrome: A chemical that forms when old red blood cells are broken down in the body. This chemical is a part of urine, and it gives urine its yellow color.

Uvula: A tissue that hangs in the back of the mouth and forms part of the soft palate. When you swallow, the uvula rises and covers the passage to your nasal cavity. This prevents food or drink from going up into your nose. If you laugh or snort when you swallow, however, the uvula may not close properly, allowing your drink to squirt out of your nose.

Vitamins: Nutrients that our bodies need in small amounts to function normally. Our bodies cannot make them, so we must get them from the food we eat. Common vitamins that are important to our health include A, B_{12}, D, C, and K.

Wolf spiders: These hunting spiders are half an inch to two inches long and do not spin webs. Wolf spiders are found all over the world. They commonly live inside houses in the fall and winter, and outside in spring and summer.

FOR MORE INFORMATION

Check out some great videos about the digestive system, part of a wonderful series called *Science Trek* (produced by Idaho PTV and streamed on the PBS LearningMedia website):

mpt.pbslearningmedia.org/resource/3ffc6955-3012-4169-9587-ddbb8ad1c49a/digestive-system-science-trek/#.WcWKDPOGO9I

DK Find Out! has a great interactive website about the digestive system (take their quiz near the bottom of the main page to find out how much you've learned!):

dkfindout.com/us/human-body/digestion

Take a "juicy journey through your digestive system" with National Geographic Kids! This website comes out of the UK, so they spell some scientific words differently than we do, and they use the metric system. For example, you'll notice that they spell esophagus "oesophagus," and that the length of the small intestine is written as "6.5 metres" instead of "21 feet":

natgeokids.com/uk/discover/science/general-science/digestive-system

This video shows the swallow reflex and a bit about the stomach:

watchknowlearn.org/Video.aspx?VideoID=3558&CategoryID=1881

This is a nice video of how the bladder signals the brain:

umms.org/ummc/patients-visitors/health-library/medical-encyclopedia/animations/bladder-function-neurological-control

References and Additional Reading

Ågren, Erik. "Blue Urine." *Newsletter of the Wildlife Disease Association, Nordic Section*. January–March, 2010. Accessed June 11, 2015. wildlifedisease.org/wda/Portals/0/WDANewsletterApril2010.pdf.

Arnold, Carrie. "Caterpillar's Bad Breath Scares Off Predators." National Geographic Ideas and Insight from Explorers. December 30, 2013. Accessed June 9, 2014. newswatch.nationalgeographic.com/2013/12/30/caterpillars-bad-breath-scares-off-predators.

Aronson, Dina. "Cortisol—Its Role in Stress, Inflammation, and Indications for Diet Therapy." *Today's Dietitian* 11.11 (2009): 38.

Arumugam, Nadia. "Food Explainer: Why Does Eating Hot Chilies Make My Nose Run?" www.slate.com, October 22, 2012. Accessed April 20, 2015. slate.com/blogs/browbeat/2012/10/22/symptoms_of_eating_hot_chilies_why_peppers_make_your_mouth_burn_nose_run.html.

Aveling, E. M. "Chew, Chew, That Ancient Chewing Gum. A Slovenly Modern Habit? Or One of the World's Oldest Pastimes." *British Archaeology* 21.6 (1997).

Bailen, Laurence. "Why Does My Stomach Growl and Make Noises?" Tufts Now, Ask the Expert. October 17, 2013. now.tufts.edu/articles/why-does-my-stomach-growl-and-make-noises. Retrieved October 27, 2014.

Bittel, Jason. "How Do Porcupines Mate? Very Carefully." slate.com, Science. November 23, 2012. Accessed November 10, 2016. slate.com/articles/health_and_science/science/2012/11/porcupine_sex_mating_behaviors_involve_quills_musk_penis_spikes_fights_and.html.

Borges, Renee M. "Of Pungency, Pain, and Naked Mole Rats: Chili Peppers Revisited." *Journal of Biosciences* 34.3 (September 2009): 349–51.

Bowen, R. "Gastrointestinal Transit: How Long Does It Take?" Control of Digestive System Function. May 27, 2006. Accessed November 10, 2016. vivo.colostate.edu/hbooks/pathphys/digestion/basics/transit.html.

Bowen, R. "Rumen Physiology and Rumination." Digestive Physiology of Herbivores. November 2009. vivo.colostate.edu/hbooks/pathphys/digestion/herbivores/rumination.html. Retrieved June 16, 2014.

Bradley, Robert M., Hideyuki Fukami, and Takeshi Suwabe. "Neurobiology of the Gustatory-Salivary Reflex." *Chemical Senses* 30.suppl 1 (2005): i70–i71.

Bredenoord, Albert J. "Aerophagia and Belching." *Practical Manual of Gastroesophageal Reflux Disease* (2013): 221.

Bredenoord, Albert J. "Excessive Belching and Aerophagia: Two Different Disorders." *Diseases of the Esophagus* 23.4 (2010): 347–52.

Bredenoord, Albert J., and André J.P.M. Smout. "Physiologic and Pathologic Belching." *Clinical Gastroenterology and Hepatology* 5.7 (2007): 772–75.

Bufe, Bernd, et al. "The Molecular Basis of Individual Differences in Phenylthiocarbamide and Propylthiouracil Bitterness Perception." *Current Biology* 15.4 (2005): 322–27.

Burks, Raychelle. "Chewing Gum." *Chemical and Engineering News* 85.32 (2007): 36.

Caller, Georgina, and Culum Brown. "Evolutionary Responses to Invasion: Cane Toad Sympatric Fish Show Enhanced Avoidance Learning." *PLOS One* 8.1 (2013): e54909.

Campos, Fernando A., and Linda M. Fedigan. "Urine-Washing in White-Faced Capuchins: A New Look at an Old Puzzle." *Behaviour* 150.7 (2013): 763–98.

Chaddock, G., et al. "Novel MRI Tests of Orocecal Transit Time and Whole Gut Transit Time: Studies in Normal Subjects." *Neurogastroenterology & Motility* 26.2 (2014): 205–14.

Ciaravola, Dell Rae. "Garlic May Repel Pests as Well as People." Nutrition Column, news.colostate.edu/Release/390. Accessed June 4, 2014.

Cliffe, Rebecca N., et al. "Mitigating the Squash Effect: Sloths Breathe Easily Upside Down." *Biology Letters* 10.4 (2014): 20140172.

Dawson, P., et al. "Residence Time and Food Contact Time Effects on Transfer of Salmonella Typhimurium from Tile, Wood and Carpet: Testing the Five-Second Rule." *Journal of Applied Microbiology* 102.4 (2007): 945–53.

Doel, J. J., et al. "Protective Effect of Salivary Nitrate and Microbial Nitrate Reductase Activity Against Caries." *European Journal of Oral Sciences* 112.5 (2004): 424–28.

Drewnowski, Adam, and Carmen Gomez-Carneros. "Bitter Taste, Phytonutrients, and the Consumer: A Review." *The American Journal of Clinical Nutrition* 72.6 (2000): 1424–35.

Ferro, Shaunacy. "How Fast Does an Elephant Pee?" *Popular Science*. October 1, 2013. Accessed November 10, 2016. popsci.com/article/science/how-fast-does-elephant-pee

Green, Barry. "Symposium Sessions—Neural and Behavioral Aspects of Chemical Senses: Lingual Heat and Cold Sensitivity Following Exposure to Capsaicin or Menthol." *Chemical Senses* (2005) 30 (suppl. 1): i201-i202.
———. "Why Is It That Eating Spicy, 'Hot' Food Causes the Same Physical Reactions as Does Physical Heat (Burning and Sweating, for Instance)?" Scientific American, Ask the Experts. October 21, 1999. Accessed November 10, 2016. scientificamerican.com/article/why-is-it-that-eating-spi.

Gupta, U. C., and S. C. Gupta. "Sources and Deficiency Diseases of Mineral Nutrients in Human Health and Nutrition: A Review." *Pedosphere* 24.1 (2014): 13–38. Retrieved October 29, 2014.

Hadley, Debbie. "Why Do Butterflies Gather Around Puddles?" About Education. Accessed November 10, 2016. ThoughtCo. thoughtco.com/why-do-butterflies-gather-around-puddles-1968178.

Hansanugrum, Areerat, and Sheryl A. Barringer. "Effect of Milk on the Deodorization of Malodorous Breath After Garlic Ingestion." *Journal of Food Science* 75.6 (2010): C549–C558.

Hays, Jeffrey. "Swiftlets and Bird's Nest Soup." 2008. Accessed December 4, 2015. factsanddetails.com/asian/cat68/sub435/item2429.html

Healthline Editorial Team. "BodyMaps: Esophagus." Accessed September 22, 2017. healthline.com/human-body-maps/esophagus.

Heaton, K. W., et al. "Defecation Frequency and Timing, and Stool Form in the General Population: A Prospective Study." *Gut* 33.6 (1992): 818–24.

Hirshon, Bob. "Nonstick Chewing Gum." AAAS Science Net Links. sciencenetlinks.com/science-news/science-updates/nonstick-chewing-gum. Retrieved October 29, 2014.

Imfeld, T. "Chewing Gum—Facts and Fiction: A Review of Gum-Chewing and Oral Health." *Critical Reviews in Oral Biology & Medicine* 10.3 (1999): 405–19.

Jiang, Peihua, et al. "Major Taste Loss in Carnivorous Mammals." *Proceedings of the National Academy of Sciences* 109.13 (2012): 4956–61.

Johnson, Meg E., and Jelle Atema. "The Olfactory Pathway for Individual Recognition in the American Lobster, *Homarus americanus.*" *Journal of Experimental Biology* 208.15 (2005): 2865–72.

Karavanich, Christa, and Jelle Atema. "Olfactory Recognition of Urine Signals in Dominance Fights Between Male Lobster, *Homarus americanus.*" *Behaviour* 135.6 (1998): 719–30.

Krishna, Aradhna, Maureen Morrin, and Eda Sayin. "Smellizing Cookies and Salivating: A Focus on Olfactory Imagery." *Journal of Consumer Research* 41.1 (2014): 18–34.

Kumar, Pavan, et al. "Natural History-Driven, Plant-Mediated RNAi-Based Study Reveals CYP6B46's Role in a Nicotine-Mediated Antipredator Herbivore Defense." *Proceedings of the National Academy of Sciences* 111.4 (2014): 1245–52.

Laitman, Jeffrey T., and Joy S. Reidenberg. "Specializations of the Human Upper Respiratory and Upper Digestive Systems as Seen Through Comparative and Developmental Anatomy." *Dysphagia* 8.4 (1993): 318–25.

Lang, I. M., B. K. Medda, and R. Shaker. "Mechanisms or Reflexes Induced by Esophageal Distension." *American Journal of Physiology-Gastrointestinal and Liver Physiology* 281: G1246–G1263, 2001.

Lennard-Jones, J. E. "Pathophysiology of Constipation." *British Journal of Surgery* 72.S1 (1985): s7–s8.

Li, Xia, et al. "Cats Lack a Sweet Taste Receptor." *The Journal of Nutrition* 136.7 (2006): 1932S–1934S.

Logemann, J. "Structural and Functional Aspects of Normal and Disordered Swallowing." In *Introduction to Organic and Neurogenic Disorders of Communication*, edited by Carole T. Ferrand and Ronald L. Bloom, 229–46. Boston: Allyn & Bacon Publishers, 1997.

The Magnificent Monarch Butterfly. "Everything There Is to Know About Monarch Butterflies." Accessed September 22, 2017. themagnificentmonarch butterfly.weebly.com/identifying-monarchs.html.

Malcolm, S. B., and L. P. Brower. "Evolutionary and Ecological Implications of Cardenolide Sequestration in the Monarch Butterfly." *Experientia* 45.3 (1989): 284–95.

Mallory, Mark L., and Mark R. Forbes. "Nest Shelter Predicts Nesting Success but Not Nesting Phenology or Parental Behaviors in High Arctic Northern Fulmars *Fulmarus glacialis.*" *Journal of Ornithology* 152.1 (2011): 119–26.

Dr. Marks. "Why Does the Stomach 'Growl' or Make Noises?" MedicineNet.com, Ask the Experts. www.medicinenet.com/script/main/art.asp?articlekey=77935. Retrieved October 29, 2014.

Martini, F. H., W. C. Ober, E. F. Bartholomew, and J. L. Nath. *Visual Essentials of Anatomy & Physiology.* Pearson Education, 2012. New York City, 2012.

Matson, John. "Fact or Fiction?: Chewing Gum Takes Seven Years to Digest." scientificamerican.com/article/fact-or-fiction-chewing-gum-takes-seven-years-to-digest. Retrieved October 20, 2014.

Matsunami, Hiroaki, and Hubert Amrein. "Taste and Pheromone Perception in Mammals and Flies." *Genome Biol* 4.7 (2003): 220.

Mayo Clinic Staff. "Bloating, Belching and Intestinal Gas: How to Avoid Them." Accessed December 4, 2015. mayoclinic.org/diseases-conditions/gas-and-gas-pains/in-depth/gas-and-gas-pains/art-20044739.

McGowan, Kat. "The Biology of . . . Saliva." *Discover*, October 2005. Accessed December 4, 2015. discovermagazine.com/2005/oct/the-biology-of-saliva#.UzA_gK1dWD8.

Mennella, Julie A. "Ontogeny of Taste Preferences: Basic Biology and Implications for Health." *The American Journal of Clinical Nutrition* 99.3 (2014): 704S–711S.

Mennella, J. A., M. Y. Pepino, F. F. Duke, and D. R. Reed. "Age Modifies the Genotype-Phenotype Relationship for the Bitter Receptor TAS2R38." *BMC Genetics* 11:60 (2010).

Menno J. Oudhoff, Jan G. M. Bolscher, Kamran Nazmi, Hakan Kalay, Wim van 't Hof, Arie V. Nieuw Amerongen, and Enno C. I. Veerman. "Histatins Are the Major Wound-Closure Stimulating Factors in Human Saliva as Identified in a Cell Culture Assay." *The FASEB Journal*, July 23, 2008.

Milov, David E., et al. "Chewing Gum Bezoars of the Gastrointestinal Tract." *Pediatrics* 102.2 (1998): e22–e22.

Mitchell, D., A. Jones, and J-M Hero. "Predation on the Cane Toad (*Bufo marinus*) by the Black Kite (*Milvus migrans*)." Memoirs of the Queensland Museum 38:2 (1995): 512.

Mitchell, S. C. "Food Idiosyncrasies: Beetroot and Asparagus." *Drug Metabolism and Disposition* 29.4 (2001): 539–43.

Mittal, Ravinder. "Motor Function of the Pharynx, Esophagus, and Its Sphincters." *Colloquium Series on Integrated Systems Physiology: From Molecule to*

Function. Vol. 3. No. 3. San Rafael, CA: Morgan & Claypool Life Sciences, 2011.

Monaenkova, Daria Matthew et al. "Butterfly Proboscis: Combining a Drinking Straw with a Nanosponge Facilitated Diversification of Feeding Habits." *Journal of the Royal Society Interface*. DOI: 10.1098/rsif.2011.0392. Published September 7, 2011.

Montagu, Ashley. *Touching: The Human Significance of the Skin*. New York: William Morrow Paperbacks, 1986.

Munch, Ryan, and Sheryl A. Barringer. "Deodorization of Garlic Breath Volatiles by Food and Food Components." *Journal of Food Science* 79.4 (2014): C526–C533.

Nasrawi, Christina Wu, and Rose Marie Pangborn. "Temporal Effectiveness of Mouth-Rinsing on Capsaicin Mouth-Burn." *Physiology & Behavior* 47.4 (1990): 617–23.

Negishi, Osamu, and Yukiko Negishi. "Enzymatic Deodorization with Raw Fruits, Vegetables and Mushrooms." *Food Science and Technology Research* 5.2 (1999): 176–80.

"Nicotine and Tobacco." medlineplus.gov/ency/article/000953.htm. Accessed May 2015.

Pappas, Stephanie. "Facts about Sulfur." Live Science, 2014. Accessed December 4, 2015. livescience.com/28939-sulfur.html.

Pelchat, M. L., C. Bykowski, F. F. Duke, and D. R. Reed. "Excretion and Perception of a Characteristic Odor in Urine after Asparagus Ingestion: A Psychophysical and Genetic Study." *Chemical Senses*, 2010. DOI: 10.1093/chemse/bjq081.

Phillips, Kimberley A., et al. "Why Do Capuchin Monkeys Urine Wash? An Experimental Test of the Sexual Communication Hypothesis Using fMRI." *American Journal of Primatology* 73.6 (2011): 578–84.

"Proboscis." Def. 2. Merriam Webster Online, Merriam Webster n.d. merriam-webster.com/dictionary/proboscis.

Rodahl, K., and T. Moore. "The Vitamin A Content and Toxicity of Bear and Seal Liver." *Biochemical Journal*, 37.2 (1943): 166–68.

Roze, Uldis. *Porcupines: The Animal Answer Guide*. Baltimore: Johns Hopkins University Press, 2012.

Saladin, Kenneth S. *Anatomy & Physiology: The Unity of Form and Function*, 5th ed. New York: McGraw-Hill, 2010.

Sampselle, Carolyn M., et al. "Continence for Women: Evidence-Based Practice." *Journal of Obstetric, Gynecologic, & Neonatal Nursing* 26.4 (1997): 375–85.

San Diego Zoo Staff. "Flamingo." San Diego Zoo Animals. animals.sandiegozoo.org/animals/flamingo. Accessed June 18, 2014.

Scully, C., S. Porter, and J. Greenman. "What to Do about Halitosis." *BMJ: British Medical Journal* 308.6923 (1994): 217.

Shabani, S., M. Kamio, and C. D. Derby. "Spiny Lobsters Use Urine-Borne Olfactory Signaling and Physical Aggressive Behaviors to Influence Social Status of Conspecifics." *Journal of Experimental Biology.* 212 (2009): 2464–74.

Shaker, R., J. Ren, M. Kern, W. J. Dodds, W. J. Hogan, and Q Li. "Mechanisms of Airway Protection and Upper Esophageal Sphincter Opening During Belching." *American Journal of Physiology-Gastrointestinal and Liver Physiology* 262: G621–G628, 1992.

Skelhorn, John, and Candy Rowe. "Distastefulness as an Antipredator Defence Strategy." *Animal Behaviour* 78.3 (2009): 761–66.

Skog, Malin. "Sex and Violence in Lobsters: A Smelly Business." Diss., Boston University, 2008.

Sobol, Jennifer. "Urinary Incontinence." University of Maryland Medical Center website, Medical Encyclopedia. 2014. Accessed November 10, 2016. umm .edu/Health/Medical/Ency/Articles/Urinary-incontinence.

Staff of Asian Nature Conservation Foundation. "Elephant Anatomy and Physiology." ANCF 2011. asiannature.org/know-elephant/elephant-anatomy -and-physiology. Retrieved 2011.

Staff of Learn about Nature. "The King of the Butterflies: The Monarch Butterfly." Learn about Nature. Accessed November 10, 2016. monarch-butterfly.com.

Stanley, Halina. "Materials Science to the Rescue: Easily Removable Chewing Gum." scienceinschool.org/print/594. Retrieved October 29, 2014.

Stegemann, Eileen. "Blue Snow." *New York State Conservationist*, February 2010.

Strom, Brian L., Ann L. Yaktine, and Maria Oria, eds. *Sodium Intake in Populations: Assessment of Evidence*. Washington, D.C.: National Academies Press, 2013.

Suarez, F., et al. "Differentiation of Mouth Versus Gut as Site of Origin of Odoriferous Breath Gases after Garlic Ingestion." *American Journal of Physiology-Gastrointestinal and Liver Physiology* 276.2 (1999): G425–G430.

Szarka, Larry, and Michael Levitt. "Belching, Bloating and Flatulence." *American College of Gastroenterology* (2006).

Tewksbury, Joshua J., and Gary P. Nabhan. "Directed Deterrence by Capsaicin in Chillies." *Nature*, vol. 412, issue 6845 (July 26, 2001): 403–404.

Thie, N. M., et al. "The Significance of Saliva During Sleep and the Relevance of Oromotor Movements." *Sleep Medicine Reviews* 6.3 (2002): 213–27.

Thompson, W. Grant. "A Noisy Tummy: What Does It Mean?" *International Foundation for Functional Gastrointestinal Disorders*. Publication # 234. June 19, 2014. iffgd.org/symptoms-causes/abdominal-noises.html.

Tominaga, Makoto. "Molecular Mechanisms of Trigeminal Nociception and Sensation of Pungency." *Chemical Senses* 30.suppl 1 (2005): i191–i192.

Vorvick, Linda. "Bladder Function: Neurological Control." University of Maryland Medical Center website, Medical Encyclopedia. 2011. Accessed November 10, 2016. umm.edu/health/medical/ency/animations/bladder-function-neurological-control.

Wong, David T. "Systemic Assessments Utilizing Saliva, Part 1: General Considerations and Current Assessments." *International Journal of Prosthodontics.* 2005: 19:43–52.

Wyman, J. B., et al. "Control of Belching by the Lower Oesophageal Sphincter." *Gut* 31.6 (1990): 639–46.

Yang, P. J., J. Pham, J. Choo, and D. L. Hu. "Duration of Urination Does Not Change with Body Size." *Proceedings of the National Academy of Sciences* 111:33 (2014): 11932–11937. doi:10.1073/pnas.1402289111.

Yarmolinsky, David A., Charles S. Zuker, and Nicholas J. P. Ryba. "Common Sense about Taste: From Mammals to Insects." *Cell* 139.2 (2009): 234–44.

INDEX